Penguin Education

Penguin English Project Stage One

Creatures Moving
Edited by Geoffrey Summerfield

Chairman: 1 ...

Penguin English Proje

Edited by Geoffrey Summerfield

tage One **Creatures Moving**

Penguin Books

Penguin Books Ltd, Harmondsworth,
Middlesex, England
Penguin Books Australia Ltd,
Ringwood, Victoria, Australia

First published 1970
Reprinted 1971
This selection copyright © Geoffrey Summerfield, 1970

Set in Monophoto Ehrhardt by
Oliver Burridge Filmsetting Ltd, Crawley, England
Printed in Great Britain by
Ebenezer Baylis & Son, Ltd., Worcester

Contents

I could have told you a lot of queer things

Now here's what a friend of mine once saw. . . . He was going home one moonlight night by a footpath through the woods when he heard a very strange noise a little distance ahead, a low whistling sound, very sharp, like the continuous twittering of a little bird with a voice like a bat, or a shrew, only softer, more musical. He went on very cautiously until he spied two hedgehogs standing in the path facing each other, with their noses almost or quite touching. He remained watching and listening to them for some moments, then tried to go a little nearer and they ran away. . . .

'But no doubt,' I said, 'you've seen other queer things in hedgehogs and in other little animals which I should like to hear.'

Yes, he had, first and last, seen a good many queer things both by day and night, in woods and other places, he replied, and then continued: 'But you see it's like this. We see something and say, "Now that's a very curious thing!" and then we forget all about it. You see, we don't lay no store by such things; we ain't scholards and don't know nothing about what's said in books. We are something and say, "*That's* something we never saw before and never heard tell of", but maybe others have seen it, and you can find it in books.
So that's how 'tis, but if I hadn't forgotten them I could have

W. H. Hudson   told you a lot of queer things.'

The Hedgehog

It is about the bigness of a Cony, but more like to a Hog, being beset and compassed all over with sharp thorny hairs, as well on the face as on the feet: and those sharp prickles are covered with a kind of soft mosse, but when she is angred or gathereth her food she striketh them up by an admirable instinct of nature, as sharp as pins or needles: these are hair at the beginning, but afterwards grow to be prickles, which is the lesse to be marvelled at, because there be Mise in Egypt which have hair like Hedge-hogs. It hath none of these prickles on the belly, and therefore, when the skin is off, it is in all parts like a Hog. . . .

His meat is Apples, Wormes, or Grapes; when he findeth apples or grapes on the earth, he rowleth himself upon them, untill he have filled all his prickles, and then carryeth them home to his den, never bearing above one in his mouth. And if it fortune that one of them fall off by the way, he likewise shaketh off all the residue, and walloweth upon them afresh, untill they be all setled upon his back again, so forth he goeth, making a noise like a cartwheele. And if he have any young ones in his nest, they pull off his load wherewithal he is loaded, eating thereof what they please, and laying up the residue for the time to come.

The History of
Four-footed Beasts
E. Topsell

Hedgehog

Twitching the leaves just where the drainpipe clogs
In ivy leaves and mud, a purposeful
Creature at night about its business. Dogs
Fear his still seriousness. He chews away

At beetles, worms, slugs, frogs. Can kill a hen
With one snap of his jaws, can taunt a snake
To death on muscled spines. Old countrymen
Tell tales of hedgehogs sucking a cow dry.

But this one, cramped by houses, fences, walls,
Must have slept here all winter in that heap
Of compost, or have inched by intervals
Through tidy gardens to this ivy bed.

And here, dim-eyed, but ears so sensitive
A voice within the house can make him freeze,
He scuffs the edge of danger; yet can live
Happily in our nights and absences.

A country creature, wary, quiet and shrewd,
He takes the milk we give him, when we're gone.
At night, our slamming voices must seem crude
To one who sits and waits for silences.

Anthony Thwaite

Hedgehogs in Heaven

The only indication of a belief in a future state which I ever
detected in an old Gypsy woman, was that she once dreamed
she was in heaven. It appeared to her as a large garden, full of
fine fat hedgehogs.

Richard Liebich

The Menagerie at
Versailles in 1775

Found Poem: Taken verbatim from a Prose Notebook kept by
Dr Samuel Johnson.

Cygnets dark; their black feet;
on the ground; tame.
Halcyons, or gulls.
Stag and hind, small.
Aviary, very large: the net, wire.
Black stag of China, small.

Rhinoceros, the horn broken
and pared away, which, I suppose,
will grow; the basis, I think,
four inches 'cross; the skin
folds like loose cloth doubled over his body
and 'cross his hips: a vast animal,
though young; as big, perhaps,
as four oxen.

kingfisher

The young elephant,
with his tusks just appearing.
The brown bear put out his paws.
All very tame. The lion.
The tigers I did not well view.
The camel, or dromedary with two bunches
called the Huguin, taller than any horse.
Two camels with one bunch.

Among the birds was a pelican,
who being let out, went
to a fountain, and swam
about to catch fish. His feet
well webbed: he dipped his head,
and turned his long bill sidewise.

John Updike

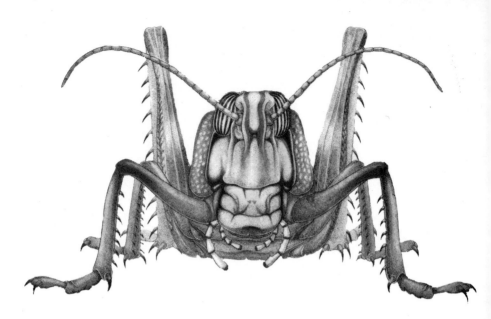

The Locust

What is a locust?
Its head, a grain of corn; its neck, the hinge of a knife;
Its horns, a bit of thread; its chest is smooth and burnished;
Its body is like a knife-handle;
Its hock, a saw; its spittle, ink;
Its underwings, clothing for the dead.
On the ground – it is laying eggs;
In flight – it is like the clouds.
Approaching the ground, it is rain glittering in the sun;
Lighting on a plant, it becomes a pair of scissors;
Walking, it becomes a razor;
Desolation walks with it.

Translated from a
Madagascan language by
A. Marre and
Willard R. Trask
Traditional

The Soft Voice of the Serpent

And then he became conscious of a curious old-mannish little face, fixed upon him in a kind of hypnotic dread. There, absolutely stilled with fear beneath his glance, crouched a very big locust. What an amusing face the thing had! A lugubrious long face, that somehow suggested a bald head, and such a glum mouth. It looked like some little person out of a Disney cartoon. It moved slightly, still looking up fearfully at him. Strange body, encased in a sort of old-fashioned creaky armour. He had never realized before what ridiculous-looking insects locusts were! Well, naturally not; they occur to one collectively, as a pest – one doesn't go around looking at their faces.

The face was certainly curiously human and even expressive, but looking at the body, he decided that the body couldn't really be called a body at all. With the face, the creature's kinship with humans ended. The body was flimsy paper stretched over a frame of matchstick, like a small boy's home-made airplane. And those could not be thought of as legs – the great saw-toothed back ones were like the parts of an old crane, and the front ones like – like one of her hairpins, bent in two. At that moment the creature slowly lifted up one of the front legs, and passed it tremblingly over its head, stroking the left antenna down. Just as a man might take out a handkerchief and pass it over his brow.

He began to feel enormously interested in the creature, and leaned over in his chair to see it more closely. It sensed him and beneath its stiff, plated sides, he was surprised to see the pulsations of a heart. How fast it was breathing . . . He leaned away a little, to frighten it less.

Watching it carefully, and trying to keep himself effaced from its consciousness by not moving, he became aware of some struggle going on in the thing. It seemed to gather itself together in muscular concentration: this co-ordinated force then passed along its body in a kind of petering tremor, and ended in a stirring along the upward shaft of the great black legs. But the locust remained where it was. Several times this wave of effort currented through it and was spent, but the next time it ended surprisingly in a few hobbling, uneven steps, undercarriage – airplanelike again – trailing along the earth.

Then the creature lay, fallen on its side, antennae turned stretched out towards him. It groped with its hands, feeling for a hold on the soft ground, bending its elbows and straining.

With a heave, it righted itself, and as it did so, he saw – leaning forward again – what was the trouble. It was the same trouble. His own trouble. The creature had lost one leg. Only the long upward shaft of its left leg remained, with a neat round aperture where, no doubt, the other half of the leg had been jointed in.

Now as he watched the locust gather itself again and again in that concentration of muscle, spend itself again and again in a message that was so puzzlingly never obeyed, he knew exactly what the creature felt. Of course he knew that feeling!
That absolute certainty that the leg was there: one had only to lift it . . . The upward shaft of the locust's leg quivered, lifted; why then couldn't he walk? He tried again. The message came; it was going through, the leg was lifting, now it was ready – now! . . . The shaft sagged in the air, with nothing, nothing to hold it up.

He laughed and shook his head: He *knew* . . . Good Lord, *exactly* like – He called out to the house – 'Come quickly! Come and see! You've got another patient!'

'What?' she shouted. 'I'm getting tea.'

'Come and look!' he called. 'Now!'

'. . . What is it?' she said, approaching the locust distastefully.

'Your locust!' he said. She jumped away with a little shriek.

'Don't worry – it can't move. It's as harmless as I am. You must have knocked its leg off when you hit out at it!' He was laughing at her.

'Oh, I didn't!' she said reproachfully. She loathed it but she loathed to hurt, even more. 'I never even touched it! All I hit was air . . . I couldn't possibly have hit it. Not its leg off.'

'All right then. It's another locust. But it's lost its leg, anyway. You should just see it. . . . It doesn't know the leg isn't there. God, I know exactly how that feels. . . . I've been watching it, and honestly, it's uncanny. I can see it feels just like I do!'

She smiled at him, sideways; she seemed suddenly pleased at something. Then, recalling herself, she came forward, bent double, hands upon her hips.

'Well, if it can't move . . .' she said, hanging over it.

'Don't be frightened,' he laughed. 'Touch it.'

'Ah, the poor thing,' she said, catching her breath in compassion. 'It can't walk.'

'Don't encourage it to self-pity,' he teased her.

She looked up and laughed. 'Oh you – ' she parried, assuming a frown. The locust kept its solemn silly face turned to her. 'Shame, isn't he a funny old man,' she said. 'But what will happen to him?'

'I don't know,' he said, for being in the same boat absolved him from responsibility or pity. 'Maybe he'll grow another one. Lizards grow new tails, if they lose them.'

'Oh, *lizards*,' she said. '– But not these. I'm afraid the cat'll get him.'

'Get another little chair made for him and you can wheel him out here with me.'

'Yes,' she laughed. 'Only for him it would have to be a kind of little cart, with wheels.'

'Or maybe he could be taught to use crutches. I'm sure the farmers would like to know that he was being kept active.'

'The poor little thing,' she said, bending over the locust again. And reaching back somewhere into an inquisitive childhood she picked up a thin wand of twig and prodded the locust, very gently. 'Funny thing is, it's even the same leg, the left one.' She looked round at him and smiled.

'I know,' he nodded, laughing. 'The two of us . . .' And then he shook his head and, smiling, said it again: 'The two of us.'

She was laughing and just then she flicked the twig more sharply than she meant to and at the touch of it there was a sudden flurried papery whirr, and the locust flew away.

She stood there with the stick in her hand, half afraid of it again, and appealed, unnerved as a child, 'What happened? What happened?'

There was a moment of silence.

'Don't be a fool,' he said irritably.

Nadine Gordimer   They had forgotten that locusts can fly.

Capturing a Fox An animal I never succeeded in keeping alive is the fox. I was always frustrated: twice by a farmer, who killed cubs I had caught before I could get to them, and once by a poultry keeper who freed my cub while his dog waited. Years after those events I was sitting up late one snowy night in dreary lodgings in London. I had written nothing for a year or so but that night I got the idea I might write something and I wrote in a few minutes the following poem: the first 'animal' poem I ever wrote. Here it is – *The Thought-Fox*.

I imagine this midnight moment's forest:
Something else is alive
Beside the clock's loneliness
And this blank page where my fingers move,

Through the window I see no star:
Something more near
Though deeper within darkness
Is entering the loneliness:

Cold, delicately as the dark snow,
A fox's nose touches twig, leaf;
Two eyes serve a movement, that now
And again now, and now, and now

Sets neat prints into the snow
Between trees, and warily a lame
Shadow lags by stump and in hollow
Of a body that is bold to come

Across clearings, an eye,
A widening deepening greenness,
Brilliantly, concentratedly,
Coming about its own business

Till, with a sudden sharp hot stink of fox
It enters the dark hole of the head.
The window is starless still; the clock ticks,
The page is printed.

This poem does not have anything you could easily call a
meaning. It is about a fox, obviously enough, but a fox that is
both a fox and not a fox. What sort of a fox is it that can step
right into my head where presumably it still sits . . . smiling to
itself when the dogs bark. It is both a fox and a spirit. It is a
real fox; as I read the poem I see it move, I see it setting its
prints, I see its shadow going over the irregular surface of the
snow. The words show me all this, bringing it nearer and
nearer. It is very real to me. The words have made a body for it
and given it somewhere to walk.

If, at the time of writing this poem, I had found livelier words,
words that could give me much more vividly its movements,
the twitch and craning of its ears, the slight tremor of its
hanging tongue and its breath making little clouds, its teeth
bared in the cold, the snow-crumbs dropping from its pads as it
lifts each one in turn, if I could have got the words for all this,
the fox would probably be even more real and alive to me now,
than it is as I read the poem. Still, it is there as it is. If I had
not caught the real fox there in the words I would never have
saved the poem. I would have thrown it into the wastepaper
basket as I have thrown so many other hunts that did not get
what I was after. As it is, every time I read the poem the fox
comes up again out of the darkness and steps into my head.
And I suppose that long after I am gone, as long as a copy of
the poem exists, every time anyone reads it the fox will get up
somewhere out in the darkness and come walking towards them.

Poetry in the Making
Ted Hughes

Mass Killings A fox *must* have an ingrained habit to kill on sight because, clearly, in lean times it just cannot afford to lose the chance of a meal by hesitating even for a split second. It is this that leads to the apparently senseless mass killing on those rare occasions when a sheer abundance of easy prey tempts it willy-nilly to an orgy of destruction. Under certain conditions, e.g. a foggy or a stormy night, the commotion of a sea-bird colony may set him off: next morning the ground littered with corpses calls to mind the slaughter in a fox raid on a chicken-house.

The carcass of this Black-headed Gull was found on the shore

and the tracks were followed back. Rounding a corner while trotting home along high-tide mark the fox had spotted a lone roosting gull. Turning sharply the fox had galloped straight towards it, as shown by the track running in from the right upper corner – its last footprint appears again in the close-up of the point of impact above.

The skids of the fox's headlong slide lead straight to the gull's two footprints, unsuspectingly facing the onslaught. The gull must have been either asleep or sick: it probably never knew what hit it!

Tracks
N. Tinbergen

In the year 1675, about half-way through September (being busy with studying air, when I had much compressed it by means of water), I discovered living creatures in rain, which had stood but a few days in a new tub, that was painted blue within. This observation provoked me to investigate this water more narrowly; and especially because these little animals were, to my eye, more than ten thousand times smaller than the animalcule which Swammerdam has portrayed, and called by the name of Water-flea, or Water-louse, which you can see alive and moving in water with the bare eye.

Of the first sort that I discovered in the said water, I saw, after divers observations, that the bodies consisted of 5, 6, 7, or 8 very clear globules, but without being able to discern any membrane or skin that held these globules together, or in which they were inclosed. When these animalcules bestirred 'emselves, they sometimes stuck out two little horns, which were continually moved, after the fashion of a horse's ears. The part between these little horns was flat, their body else being roundish, save only that it ran somewhat to a point at the hind end; at which pointed end it had a tail, near four times as long as the whole body, and looking as thick, when viewed through my microscope, as a spider's web. At the end of this tail there was a pellet, of the bigness of one of the globules of the body; and this tail I could not perceive to be used by them for their movements in very clear water. These little animals were the most wretched creatures that I have ever seen; for when, with the pellet, they did but hit on any particles or little filaments (of which there are many in water, especially if it hath but stood some days), they stuck intangled in them; and then pulled their body out into an oval, and did struggle, by stretching themselves, to get their tail loose; whereby their whole body then sprang back towards the pellet of the tail, and their tails then coiled up serpent-wise, after the fashion of a copper or iron wire that, having been wound close about a round stick, and then taken off, kept all its windings. This motion, of stretching out and pulling together the tail, continued; and I have seen several hundred animalcules, caught fast by one another in a few filaments, lying within the compass of a coarse grain of sand.

Anthony van
Leeuwenhoek

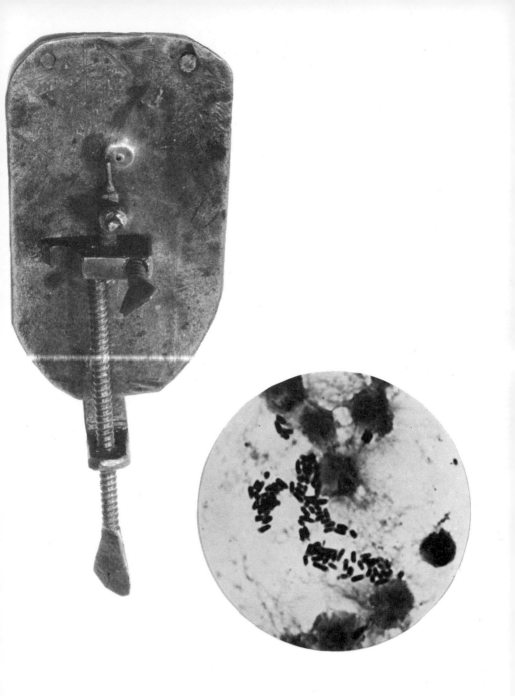

Observing Flies In the decline of the year, when the mornings and evenings became chilly, many species of flies *[Muscae]* retire into houses, and swarm in the windows.

At first they are very brisk and alert; but as they grow more torpid, one cannot help observing that they move with difficulty, and are scarce able to lift their legs, which seem as if glued to the glass; and by degrees many do actually stick on till they die in the place.

It has been observed that divers flies, besides their sharp hooked nails, have also skinny palms, or flaps to their feet, whereby they are enabled to stick on glass and other smooth bodies, and to walk on ceilings with their backs downward, by means of the pressure of the atmosphere on those flaps; the weight of which they easily overcome in warm weather when they are brisk and alert. But in the decline of the year, this resistance becomes too mighty for their diminished strength; and we see flies labouring along, and lugging their feet in windows, as if they stuck fast to the glass, and it is with the utmost difficulty they can draw one foot after another, and disengage their hollow caps from the slippery surface.

Upon the same principle that flies stick and support themselves, do boys, by way of play, carry heavy weights by only a piece of wet leather at the end of a string clapped close on the surface of

Gilbert White a stone.

The Fly It hath wings, not such as other things that flie have, but made of little skins as the Locusts, Grasshoppers and Bees are, but a very great deal softer, as an Indian Garment is softer than those of Greece. If any man observe the Fly when he opens his wings in the Sun, he may perceive them painted with variety of colours, as the Peacocks are. He doth not flie straight forward, as the Bats do; nor skipping as the Locusts, nor making a noyse as the Wasp; but winding in and out to what part of the air soever he pleaseth to move himself. Neither doth he flie quietly and in silence but with singing and melody; not so hardhearted and cruel as the gnat or little Flyes, not as Bees and Wasps with a grave harshnesse, making a horrible and terrible murmuring; yea so far doth the Fly exceed all these in

The History sweetness of sound as he flieth, as the small Pipe doth the
of Four-footed Beasts Trumpet and Cymbal, or as still musick is sweeter than the
T. Muffet loud.

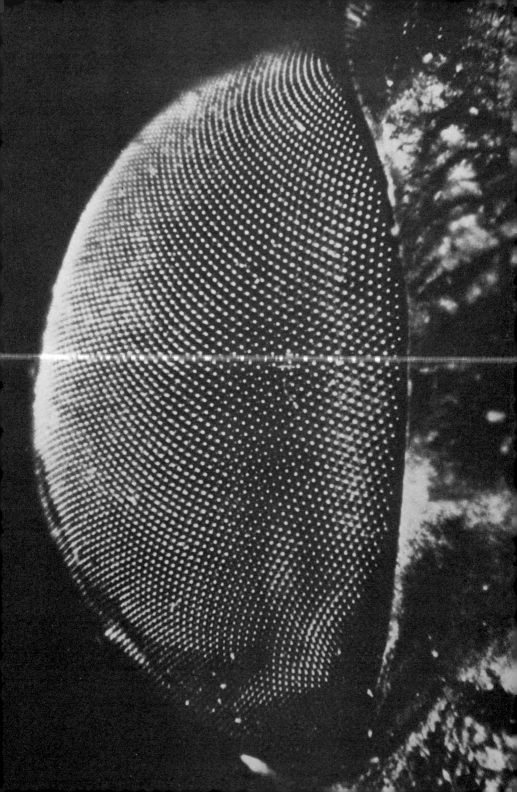

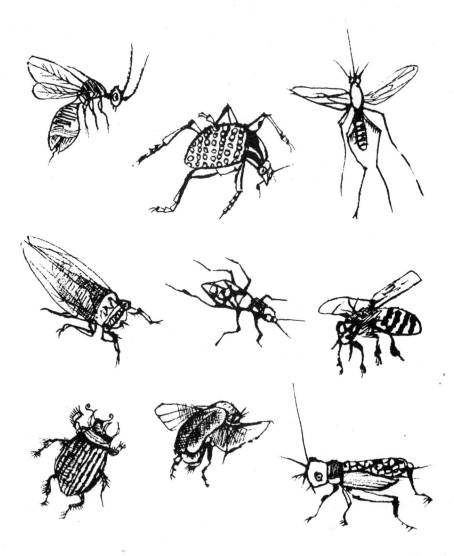

The Naming of Insects

It is most important to be a good namer, since it falls to us all at some time or other to name anything from a canary to a castle, and since names generally have to last a long time. Here are some possible names for insects, to give you ideas.

Alastair Reid

1 TWILLITER	4 LIMLET	7 THRIMM
2 FLURR	5 TILLTIN	8 LEGLIDDY
3 TRISTRAM	6 SUMMERSBY	9 UGWOB

At the Housefly Planet

Upon the housefly planet
the fate of the human is grim:
for what he does here to the housefly,
the fly does there unto him.

To paper with honey cover
the humans there adhere,
while others are doomed to hover
near death in vapid beer.

Translated from the German by Max Knight
Christian Morgenstern

However, one practice of humans
the flies will not undertake:
they will not bake us in muffins
nor swallow us by mistake.

William Blake

The wanton boy that kills the fly
Shall feel the spider's enmity.

Haiku
Translated from the Japanese by R. H. Blyth
Wafû

We listen to insects,
And human voices,
With different ears.

2

3

6

A Chorale of Cherokee Night Music
As Heard Through an Open Window
in Summer Long Ago

screech owl, hoot owl, yellow-breasted chat, jar-fly, cricket, carolina chickadee,
katydid, crow, wolf, beetle, turkey, goose, bullfrog, spring frog

wahuhu wahuhu wahuhu wahuhu wahuhu wahuhu wa

uguku uguku uguku uguku uguku uguku uguku uguku

huhu huhu huhu huhu huhu huhu huhu huhu huhu hu

lalu lalu lalu lalu lalu lalu lalu lalu lalu lalu lalu lalu lalu

talatu talatu talatu talatu talatu talatu talatu talatu talatu

tsikilili tsikilili tsikilili tsikilili tsikilili tsikilili tsikilili tsikil

tsikiki tsikiki tsikiki tsikiki tsikiki tsikiki tsikiki tsikiki ts

kagu kagu kagu kagu kagu kagu kagu kagu kagu kagu

waya waya waya waya waya waya waya waya waya way

yeah yeah yeah yeah yeah yeah yeah yeah yeah yeah ye

guna guna guna guna guna guna guna guna guna gun

sasa sasa sasa sasa sasa sasa sasa sasa sasa sasa sa

kununu kununu kununu kununu kununu kununu kunu

dustu dustu dustu dustu dustu dustu dustu dustu dus

Jonathan Williams

Orgy
Edwin Morgan

```
c a n t e r c a n t e r c a n t e r c a n t e r
a n t e a t e r a n t e a t e r a n t e a t e r
a n t e n c o u n t e r a n t e n c o u n t e r
a n t e n n a r e a c t a n t e n n a r e a c t
a n t a n t a n t a n t a n t a n t a n t a n t
a n t a n t a n t a n t a n t a n t a n t a n t
a n t a n t a n t a n t a n t a n t a n t a n t
a n t a n t a n t a n t a n t a n t a n t a n t
c a n t c o u n t a n t c a n t c o u n t a n t
a n a c c o u n t a n a c c o u n t a n t
a n t e a t e r a n t e a t e r a n t e a t e r
e a t e a t e a t e a t e a t e a t e a t e a t
e a t e a t e a t e a t e a t e a t e a t e a t
a n t e a t e n a n t e a t e n a n t e a t e n
n e c t a r n e c t a r n e c t a r n e c t a r
t r a n c e t r a n c e t r a n c e t r a n c e
* * * * * * * * * * * * * * *
c a n t e a t a n a n t c a n t e a t a n a n t
a n t e a t e r c a n t a n t e a t e r c a n t
n o t a n a n t n o t a n a n t n o t a n a n t
* * * * * * * * * * * * * * *
t r a n c e t r a n c e t r a n c e t r a n c e
o c o n t e n t o c o n t e n t o c o n t e n t
n o c a n t e r n o c a n t e r n o c a n t e r
```

Boy and a Butterfly

A stunted oak
Cast no shadow beneath a sun-rare sky,
It creaked,
As if at any moment this lazy breeze
Might send it
Tumbling to the bottom of a neighbouring stream.
The tree bowed towards an idle river,
Slowly wandering to the sea.
The blue-grey sky did not contrast with the scenery.
Distantly the horizon was vague, in shades of blue,
And the water of silver-grey
Glittered in the cold mist, planished in white diamonds,
Like the ivory keys of a piano,
Dancing madly up and down.
The breeze broke without warning
Into tantrums of whistling wind,
Tossing the sparse foliage,
And sweeping the long, faded, rank grass, like waves on an ocean.
Above that swaying sheet
Hovered on paper-like wings,
Tinged at the edges with the palest shade of lemon,
A butterfly.
Two bright blue eyes caught a glimpse of this airborne wonder,
And a barefoot boy shouted with delight.
With his short plump fingers stretched out
He reached hopefully up into the sky,
Chasing carelessly,
With jerking legs, through the coarse grass,
Stamping it down as he ran.
Wide-eyed, he gazed and followed its every movement.
Along the riverbank he ran,
Jumping up and down, as the wind blew through his hair,
Jumping, and rolling on the ground,
And laughing as he did.
Until at last he poked his head above the swaying stalks;
And that butterfly had gone.
He stared into the distance,

Age 14   Searchingly, longingly,
Phillip Chappell   But it was gone.

Talking to a Butterfly

Rudyard Kipling

There was never a king like Solomon
Not since the world began
Yet Solomon talked to a butterfly
As a man would talk to a man.

Haiku
Translated from the Japanese by R. H. Blyth
Garaku

The butterfly,
Even when pursued,
    Never appears in a hurry.

Goldwing Moth

Carl Sandburg

A Goldwing moth is between the scissors and the ink bottle on the desk.
Last night it flew hundreds of circles around a glass bulb and a flame wire.
The wings are a soft gold; it is the gold of illuminated initials in manuscripts of the medieval monks.

Haiku
Translated from the Japanese by R. H. Blyth
Issa

An exhausted sparrow
In the midst
    Of a crowd of children

Haiku
Translated from the Japanese by R. H. Blyth
Otsuyu

The swallow
Turns a somersault;
    What has it forgotten?

Haiku
Translated from the Japanese by R. H. Blyth
Yayu

Sneezing,
I lost sight
    Of the skylark

Feel Like A Bird

feel like A Bird
understand
he has no hand

instead A Wing
close-lapped
mysterious thing

in sleeveless coat
he halves The Air
skipping there
like water-licked boat

lands on star-toes
finger-beak in
feather-pocket
finds no coin

in neat head like
seeds in A Quartered
Apple eyes join
sniping at opposites
stereoscope The Scene
Before

close to floor giddy
no arms to fling
A Third Sail
spreads for calm
his tail

hand better
than A Wing?
to gather A Heap
to count
to clasp A Mate?

or leap
lone-free and mount
on muffled shoulders
May Swenson   to span A Fate?

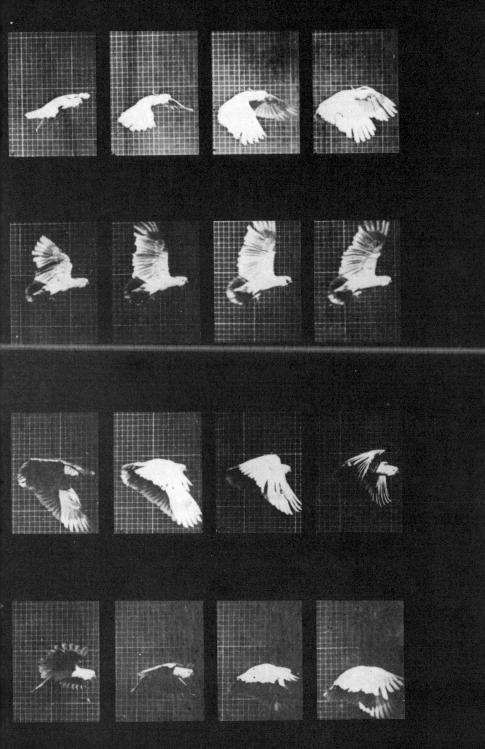

Heron

delver

A gawky stilt-
ed fossicker a-
mong reeds, the
gun-grey-green
one, gauntly
watchful cold-
eye, stiff on
single column a
brooding hump
of wind-ruffled
feather-brain
feathering the
blue shall-
ows with one
scaly claw
poised drip-
ping –

    wades
the pebbled lake,
prints the mudflat,
scorns the noi-
sy fancy oy-
stercatchers' talk,
stalks, tall, to
his flat ramshack-
le nest or shack
of slack sticks
with three dull
greeny eggs
by a bul-
rush grove –

till the snaky neck
coils back
and strikes, beak
darts and spears
quick fish,
fish, fish
silvery-rich
fisher-king dish –

and then in the lone-
ly white lazy
hazy afternoon

he rises slowly
in a big zig-
zag heavy over
sultry fens
and windmill vanes,
flapping silently
Edwin Morgan   in the land of wings.

The Raven

Tracks
N. Tinbergen

Toughness, versatility, and intelligence tide the Raven through the Arctic winter. It lives on seal-carcasses left by polar bears. It hunts ptarmigan, guillemots, and other birds and has even been seen chiselling fish out of fjord ice. Here a raven has alighted in deep snow, leaving a dramatic spread of wing and tail before wading on thigh-deep to investigate whatever took its fancy.

Rook-Shooting

The men had been rook-shooting all the morning among the elms of Doldylyn. After luncheon they asked me to go out with them and see the shooting. I went but I did not like it and soon came away. Most of them were shooting with rifles. Trevellyn shot the best. He is a capital shot. He shot a rabbit with his beautiful little rook-rifle like a long saloon pistol. The old rooks were all scared away, sailing round at an immense height in the blue sky, and it was pitiable to see the young rooks bewildered, wheeling and fluttering helplessly from tree to tree, and perching, only to be tumbled bleeding with a dull thud into the deep nettle beds below, by the ceaseless and relentless crack crack of the beautiful cruel little rifles, or to see them stagger after the shot, hold on as long as possible and then, weak from loss of blood, stumble from their perch, and flutter down, catching at every bough, and perhaps run along the ground terrified and bewildered, in the agonies of a broken wing. It may not be cruel, but I don't

Francis Kilvert think I could ever be a sportsman.

The Fire-Engine and the Jackdaws

When I left the Cathedral after evensong all the good folks of Canterbury seemed to be in the Cathedral close and there was great excitement. The authorities had just got down a new steam fire-engine for the protection of the Cathedral from the periodical fires which threaten it, and they were throwing a jet of water over the Cathedral roof, the water seething, foaming, boiling and bubbling in the great tub round the hose as the steam from the engine rushed and roared through it. A good deal of the water fell back from the north-western tower in spray, in which the bright sunshine made a brilliant dazzling wavering sparkling rainbow arch about six feet high.

As the jet of water was playing over the Cathedral roof I watched the jackdaws disturbed from their usually quiet haunts and sailing round and round the central tower at a great height in the cloudless sky, and I marked their shadows upon the grey rich sunny Tower, how they crossed and recrossed, shrunk and grew, disappeared and appeared again, flitting softly and silently to and fro like the dim ghosts of

Francis Kilvert birds who had inhabited that same tower centuries before.

The Chaffinch
Map of Scotland
Edwin Morgan

chaffinch
chaffinchaffinch
chaffinchaffinchaffinch
chaffinchaffinchaffinch
chaffinchaffinch
chaffinch
chaffie   chye   chaffiechaffie
chaffie   chye   chaffiechaffie
chye chaffie
chaffiechaffiechaffie
chaffiechaffiechaffie
chaffiechaffie
chaffiechaffie
chaffiechaffie
chaffiechaffie

shillyshelly
shelfyshilfyshellyshilly
shelfyshillyshilly
shilfyshellyshelly
shilfyshelfyshelly
shellyfaw
shielyshellyfaw

shilfy
shilfyshelfy   shielyshiely
shilfyshelfyshelfy   shielychaffie
chaffiechaffie   chaffiechaffie
chaffiechaffie
shilfyshilfyshilfyshelfyshelfy
chaffieshilfyshilfyshelfyshelfyshelfyshelfy
chaffieshilfyshilfyshelfyshelfyshelfyshelfyshelfy
shilfyshilfyshilfyshelfy   shelfyshelfy
shilfy   shilfy
shilfy
shilfyshelfy

brichtie

Tadpole Time

Well it was once when I was a kid. I was at Junior school.
I think, or somewhere like that, and went down to Fowlers
Pond, me and this other kid. Reggie Clay they called him, he
didn't come to this school; he flitted and went away
somewhere. Anyway it was Spring, tadpole time, and it's
swarming with tadpoles down there in Spring. Edges of
t'pond are all black with 'em, and me and this other kid
started to catch 'em. It was easy, all you did, you just put
your hands together and scooped a handful of water up and
you'd got a handful of tadpoles. Anyway we were mucking
about with 'em, picking 'em up and chucking 'em back and
things, and we were on about taking some home, but we'd no
jam jars. So this kid, Reggie, says, 'Take thi wellingtons off
and put some in there, they'll be all right 'til tha gets home.'
So I took 'em off and we put some water in 'em and then we
started to put taddies in 'em. We kept ladling 'em in and I
says to this kid, 'Let's have a competition, thee have one welli'
and I'll have t'other, and we'll see who can get most in!' So he
started to fill one welli' and I started to fill t'other. We must
have been at it hours, and they got thicker and thicker, until
at t'end there was no water left in 'em, they were just jam
packed wi' taddies.

You ought to have seen 'em, all black and shiny, right up to
t'top. When we'd finished we kept dipping us fingers into 'em
and whipping 'em up at each other, all shouting and excited
like. Then this kid says to me, 'I bet tha daren't put one on.'

And I says, 'I bet thar daren't.' So we said that we'd put one on each. We wouldn't though, we kept reckoning to, then running away, so we tossed up and him who lost had to do it first. And I lost, oh, and you'd to take your socks off an' all. So I took my socks off, and I kept lookin at this welli' full of taddies, and this kid kept saying, 'Go on then, tha frightened, tha frightened.' I was an' all. Anyway I shut my eyes and started to put my foot in. Oooo. It was just like putting your foot into live jelly. They were frozen. And when my foot went down, they all came over t'top of my wellington, and when I got my foot to t'bottom, I could feel 'em all squashing between my toes.

Anyway I'd done it, and I says to this kid, 'Thee put thine on now.' But he wouldn't, he was dead scared, so I put it on instead. I'd got used to it then, it was all right after a bit; it sent your legs all excited and tingling like. When I'd got 'em both on I started to walk up to this kid, waving my arms and making spook noises; and as I walked they all came squelching over t'tops again and ran down t'sides. This kid looked frightened to death, he kept looking down at my wellies so I tried to run at him and they all spurted up my legs. You ought to have seen him. He just screamed out and ran home roaring.

A Kestrel for a Knave
Barry Hines

It was a funny feeling though when he'd gone; all quiet, with nobody there, and up to t'knees in tadpoles.

I am the slowworm

I am neither snake nor lizard,
I am the slowworm.

Ripe wheat is my lodging. I polish
part of a church   my side on pillars of its transept,
gleam in its occasional light.
Its swaying
copies my gait.

Vaults stored with slugs to relish,
my quilt a litter of husks, I prosper
lying low, little concerned.
My eyes sharpen
when I blink.

Good luck to reaper and miller!
Grubs adhere even to stubble.
Come plowtime
the ditch is near.

Sycamore seed twirling,
O, writhe to its measure!
Dust swirling scans pleasure.

Thorns prance in a gale.
In air snow flickers,
twigs tap,
elms drip.

Swaggering, shimmering fall,
Basil Bunting   drench and towel us all!

Snakes   I do not know how to class the venemous animals further then
by the vulgar notion of putting toads common snakes black
snakes – calld by the Peasantry Vipers – Newts (often called
eatherns) and a nimble scaly looking newt-like thing about the
furze-collector   heaths calld Swifts by the furze kidders and cow keepers   all
these we posses in troublsome quantitys all of which is
reckond poisonous by the common people tho a many daring
people has provd that the common snake is not for I have
seen men with whom I have workd in the fields take them up
and snatch them out of joint as they calld it in a moment so
that when they was thrown down they could not stir but lay
and dyd   others will take them up in one hand and hold the
other agen that double pointed fang which they put out in a
threatning manner when pursued and which is erroniously
calld their sting and when it touches the hand it appears
utterly harmless and turns again as weak as an horse hair   yet
still they are calld poisonous and dreaded by many people
and I myself cannot divest my feelings of their first
impressions tho I have been convincd to the contrary   we
have them about us in great quantitys   they even come in
the village and breed on the dunghills in farm yards and
harbour in old walls   they are fond of lying rolld up like a
whipthong in the sun   they seem to be always jealous of
danger as they never lye far from their hiding places and
retreat in a moment at the least noise or sound of approaching
feet   they lay a great number of eggs white and large   the
shell is a skinny substance and full of a glutiness matter like
the white in birds eggs   they hang together by hundreds as
if strung on a string   they lay them on the south side of old
dunghills were the heat of the sun and the dung together
hatches them   when they first leave the shells they are no
thicker then a worsted needle or bodkin   they nimble about
after the old snakes and if they are in danger the old ones open
their mouths and the young dissapear down their throats in a
moment till the danger is over and then they come out and
run about as usual   I have not seen this myself but I am as
certain of it as if I had because I have heard it told so often
peeling   by those that did when I have been pilling bark in the woods
in oaking time   I have seen snakes creeping half errect by
the sides of the fallen oaks that were pilld putting their
darting horse hair like tongue every now and then to the tree
and I was a long while ere I could make out what they were
doing but I made it out at last in my mind that they were
catching flyes that were attracted there in great quantitys to

the moister of the sap just after the bark had been ripd off
this I have observd many times and I think if it were examind
they have a sticky moister at the end of those double ended
fangs that appear like a bit of wailbone split at the end or a
double horse hair which attaches to the flye as soon as
touchd like bird lime and I think this is the use for which
nature designd their mistaken stings   the motion was so
quick that the prey which it seizd coud not be percievd when
taken but I have not the least doubt that such was its object
people talk about the Watersnake but I cannot believe

than otherwise then that the water and land snake are one tho I
have killd snakes by the water in meadows of a different and
more deep color then those I have founds in the fields   the
water snake will swallow very large frogs   I have often known
them to be ripd out of their bellys by those who have skind
the snake to wear the skin round their hats which is reckond
as a charm against the headach and is often tryd but with
what success I am not able to say . . . when the french
prisoners were at Norman cross Barracks it was a very common
thing among the people of the villages round to go in the fens
a snake catching and carry home large sticks of them strung
like eels on osiers which the French men woud readily buy as
an article of very palatable food . . . the common snake is very
fond of milk and it often makes its way into a dairy by a mouse
hole or some other entrance to sip the cream – in the fens
(were they are as numerous as flies) they will creep up the
milk pails that are set to cool at the door of an evening by 3

John Clare   or four together

Snake-Phobia   In the part of Australia where I grew up we used to come across snakes quite often when we were walking in the bush, and our fear and loathing of them was something more than the usual thing, mainly, I suppose, because very occasionally some of us really did get bitten. I never saw a snake – that furtive sliminess, that mad, hating eye – without a sudden instinctive constriction of the heart, and after the first moment of panic was over we children had just one thought in our minds: 'Kill it. Do not let it get away.' And so we would grab a stick and in a spasm of furious terror we would beat at the hideous twisting thing until at last it lay inert in the dust. Even then we would not dare to touch it; we would hook it up with the stick and toss it away out of sight into the long grass where ants were bound to demolish it within a day or two.

We all knew what to do if we got bitten, and most of us carried about with us a little tin box in which were one of father's razor blades and a phial of permanganate of potash crystals. First you tied your handkerchief round the arm or the leg *above* the bite and tightened it by twisting the knot with a piece of stick. This slowed the flow of the poison to the heart. Next you made an incision between the two punctures caused by the snake's fangs, and provided you had no hollow teeth you sucked out as much blood as you could. Then you rubbed the crystals into the wound, and with luck all would be well.

We knew all about snakes. There was the ferocious tiger snake that automatically attacked and could run as fast as you could. Then there were the brown snakes and the taipans and many other varieties, all of them deadly, and they lurked among rotten logs, and in the bracken and on the edges of swamps waiting to strike; and if they did strike and you did nothing about it you were dead within half an hour. The pythons and carpet-snakes were not poisonous, but they would drop on you from an overhanging branch and suffocate you by wrapping themselves around your neck. Many of the lizards were also poisonous, and those that were not inflicted a sore that continued to suppurate for years. Snakes could be calmed by music, and one way of getting them into the open so that they could be killed was to lay out a saucer of milk – a drink they could never resist.

These notions I have lived with all my life, and it never occurred to me to question them until I returned to Australia last year and spent some time with Eric Worrell, a self-taught herpetologist who runs a snake farm at a place called Gosford, which is a little to the north of Sydney in New South Wales. Now I do not suggest that my experiences at this place came to me as a revelation, that overnight my revulsion turned to love, yet it was quite a sharp shock to learn that almost everything I thought I knew about reptiles, and·had been talking about all these years, was wrong; not just inaccurate, but absolutely wrong.

Even the simplest articles of my beliefs were miles away from the truth. No Australian snake will ever attack unless it is provoked; it invariably runs away. It does this because it is an intensely frightened and fragile creature: one blow on those delicate hairpin-thin bones will instantly break its back. Its poison is its only means of self-defence, and even this is not very effective: among all the varieties of Australian snakes – and there are 140 of them – only five of them are really venomous. The rest can do no more than inflict a sting like a wasp. No lizard is poisonous and none can inflict a wound that will not heal. No python ever dropped on a man out of a tree. Snakes are quite indifferent to music (the snake charming act is a plain fraud), and they hate milk. Moreover they are not in the least slimy or clammy. If you pick one up you will find that it is warm and dry, rather like the feel of a young baby's arm or leg. They are the cleanest of all creatures and they have no smell; you can handle them all day and there is no odour whatever left on your hands.

Worrell, a stocky, bearded man with very strong arms, has about a thousand snakes which he milks for their venom. The thin, pale, golden fluid is dehydrated until it becomes a dry powder (which will keep fresh for a long time) and is ultimately made into a liquid with which horses are injected. When the horses have attained the right amount of immunity their blood is drawn off and is used by the hospitals as an anti-snake-bite serum.

I happened to go down to his farm because I was making a television film about Australian wild life, and much as I hated snakes it seemed only fair that they should be included in the show if only as the villains of the piece. The place was more or less what you might have expected: the tropical snakes in warmed, glassed-in enclosures and the others crawling around by the hundreds in open pits. The only thing that divided the onlooker from the snakes in the pits was a low concrete wall over which one leaned and felt one's flesh creep. Worrell jumped in, picked up a three-foot tiger snake by the tail, and held it out to me.

'Take it.'

'No,' I said.

'I promise it won't bite you.'

'No,' I said.

'There's nothing for you to be afraid of.'

'I don't care,' I said. 'I am not going to do it.'

Yet he was extraordinarily compelling: his confidence was infectious. While the cameras were being set up he pointed out to me a sheet of corrugated iron that was lying on a low flat mound in the sunshine.

'Under this,' he said, 'there are about forty black snakes. Now come and sit here and lift it up. It will make an excellent shot.'

'What,' I asked from my side of the wall, 'will happen?'

'They will move quietly away.'

'How?'

'Some will go off in that direction. Others will just slither across your lap and disappear.'

'No,' I said.

'You're not frightened, are you?'

'You bet I'm frightened.'

'All right. *I'll* sit here and lift the sheet of iron. You stand alongside me. I tell you, you will not be bitten.'

Strangely I felt better after I had climbed over the wall, and felt no real desire to jump back again when he lifted up the iron sheet. There they lay, black, intertwined with one another and gleaming in the sunshine, and with that kind of numbness that overtakes one in a car accident – a sense of fatalistic passivity – I watched them placidly slither away.

We did a good deal of filming that day among both the snakes and the lizards, and I found that, as time went on, I was able to go into their pits so long as Worrell was with me and preferably in front of me. But I could not bear to be left alone even when I was assured that the snakes at my feet were not venomous.

The pythons were a little disappointing since they were all coiled up asleep, and at dinner that night I said to Worrell, 'I wonder what they are doing now?'

'Let's go and see.'

On the way over to their enclosure we paused to look in on some young tiger snakes Worrell was keeping a special eye on. He picked one up and handed it to me.

'Take it.'

We had had a good dinner, and Australian wines these days are almost up to the quality of France. I took it, holding it by the tail and well out from my body, and then quickly handed it back. It was a ridiculously small incident of course, but privately I felt, with elation, that I had crossed some kind of neurotic frontier of the mind, and I went on eagerly to see the pythons.

They were housed in a series of small warmed rooms with glass fronts, and in a gentle artificial light we could see that they had uncoiled themselves from the dead logs and branches on which they had been asleep all day. Their sleek heads and perhaps as much as three or four feet of their bodies swayed to and fro through the air with a strange questing motion. It was as though they were looking beyond us, searching for something in the darkness outside. Back and forth they went in a slow compulsive rhythm. It was exceedingly beautiful and it had a mesmerising effect, an effect that is sometimes produced when one looks down into a rock pool and sees there long strands of seaweed that are drawn first this way and and then that by some invisible current.

'Come on,' Worrell said. 'Let's go inside.'

'Have they eaten?'

'As a matter of fact they have. But it wouldn't have mattered anyway.'

He unlocked the door of the cage where some half-dozen scrub pythons – it was difficult to tell just how many – were moving about. They took no notice of us at all as we stepped inside, and at least it was reassuring that they moved so deliberately and slowly. On the other side of the glass the

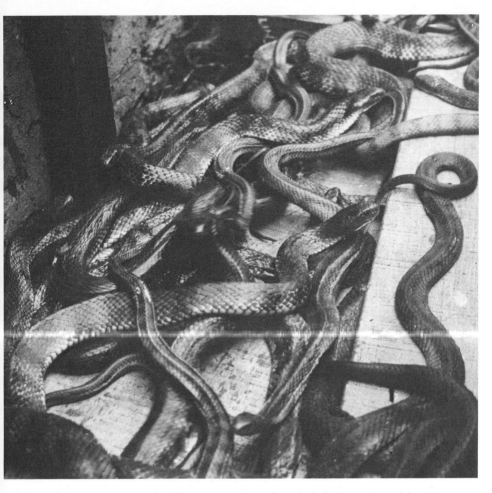

television crew were setting up their cameras, and it was an odd business being on the inside looking out. None of the cameramen smiled or waved; they simply peered at us standing there among the slowly writhing bodies as though we were part of the exhibit, and I began to have the feeling that I too ought to be swaying back and forth and putting on some sort of a show.

'Even if I angered one of them,' Worrell said, 'I could still calm it down again. Look.'

He took his handkerchief from his pocket and fluttered it before the head of the nearest python. At once it drew back its head and coiled its great neck in the form of an S, ready to strike. Worrell pocketed his handkerchief and reached his hand forward to take hold of the python behind its head. He was a little too slow. The head darted forward like a piece of elastic that had suddenly been let go, and the two cruel jaws clamped themselves on his hand between his thumb and fingers. Blood spouted out and it must have been horribly painful, but he calmly prised the jaws apart, and as the python turned away he went after it, murmuring to it, reaching forward to it, stroking it. And the python did in fact subside. Presently Worrell was able to take it up, and it coiled itself round him, settling down comfortably around his waist and shoulders.

Although I had taken no part in these proceedings I had – one searches for a phrase – a good conceit of myself at having been there in the cage and only a couple of feet away when the bite was made, and it was a little galling to discover when we emerged that the cameramen had run out of film and had recorded nothing of the incident.

Next day there was a telephone call from a farmhouse about five miles away. 'A snake got into my little boy's bedroom last night,' the woman there said. 'A big one. Now it's gone out into the shed and it's coiled around the rafters there.'

When we arrived at the farm we found an old man leaning over the gate obviously on the lookout for us. He jerked his thumb back in the direction of a large wooden shed in the yard. 'He's here,' he said.

It was a diamond python, six or seven feet long, and I found that after the experiences of the previous day I could look on it, not as an object of horror, but as a living creature: even more than that, as an object of great beauty. There were marvellous markings on its greenish-yellow head, and its diamond-patterned coils flowed round the rafter like some flowering tropical creeper that had grown up out of the ground.

The woman and the rest of the farmer's family now arrived. 'The snake is harmless,' Worrell said. 'It will not attack your little boy or any of you. On the contrary, it will do a great deal of good around the farm by killing off the vermin.'

'Take it away,' the woman said.

'You don't want rats and mice around the place do you?' Worrell said.

'Take it away.'

He got a sack out of his car and told me to hold it open while
he clambered up on to a wooden box and began to disengage
the snake from the rafter. It was very neatly done. First one
coil was loosened, then the next, and then at the right moment
he took the snake by the neck and dropped it into the sack.
I fancied I heard a sigh of relief go up from the family.

I had a fellow-feeling for that snake – it really was a very
beautiful thing – and I went back to see it in its enclosure at
Worrell's place several times that day. Snakes are very
sluggish creatures, comfort-loving and not very intelligent.
This one had coiled himself down in the warmth and was
happy. When they wanted a picture of me with a python I had
no hesitation in choosing this one. As with small babies the
thing with pythons is to hold them, not gingerly, but firmly.
In that way you give them confidence. This one wrapped
itself round me two or three times, shifted its position a little
until it was comfortable, and then went into a doze. It would
be a lie to say I was not frightened, but at least I was not in a
panic. I felt I had a certain *rapport* with the creature, and
that it was not going to bite me any more than it would have
bitten a tree on which it might have chosen to rest.

As I have said, I did not come away from Worrell's farm with
the sense of having had a revelation about snakes, but I felt
quite certainly that never again would I look on them in quite
the same way. From now on they would no longer be an
implacable evil, and I would not wish to kill them on sight.
I would know that they were not going to attack me, that they

had a place in the natural scheme of things, and that, when seen with a detached eye, one would discover that they had much beauty and much grace in all their movements. In short, the myth was broken – the myth which was compounded of so many warnings from my parents, of Kipling's horrific short story *Rikki Tikki Tavi* (the one about cobras), and of so many bad snake dreams and snake fears in my childhood. All this gave me a certain glow of satisfaction, plus, I must admit, a slight feeling of superiority.

And, of course, I was entirely wrong again. One does not recover from ingrained irrational fears quite so easily as this. Not three months after I had left Worrell I came across a little adder one day when I was walking along a dry water-course and instantly habit reasserted itself: I grabbed a stick and beat it to death.

I was sorry afterwards and excused myself on the grounds that it might have bitten someone who had inadvertently stepped upon it in the grass; but then I am not absolutely sure that I would not do the same thing again. Which leads one to the uncomfortable thought that the world must be filled with people who are convinced that mice are going to run up their legs, and that bats will get into their hair, and that spiders will always bite them, and that walls are going to close in on them, and that they are bound to jump off if they look down from a great height, and that God knows how many other fearful delusions bedevil our minds from earliest childhood and that some of us are never really going to get over them.

Alan Moorehead

The Cave

Soon I became aware of a strange high-pitched twittering sound. I looked inquiringly at my guides but they had no explanation to offer. Carefully we made our way forwards with the noise growing louder and louder, until the whole air was filled with the deafening cacophony of sound. Was there gas escaping from some vent, or was this the hum of a gigantic swarm of insects?

I tied a handkerchief over my face and entered the mouth of the cave.

Clive Spinage

A Country Matter

Out on some nature ramble with the school
I found a hole in the ground tangled with grass
And kicked it – kicked it over again to feel
The earth all round my foot. It was a wasps' nest.
They rose in droning clouds, my head was wasps,
Hands in front of my eyes I stumbled down
The hill, myself a frantic hill of wasps –
One, cleaving to my temple, drilled right in.

My cries, they told me, could have been heard for miles,
But no one came. My fellow-pupils knew
Too well what lumps came up from red-hot weals,
And teachers felt they weren't paid to rescue
Boys from self-inflicted wounds. I ran
Blindly of course, crashed down into the wood,
Splashed across the beck, then up stream bellowing,
Shaking wasps off like confetti as I went.

The last one still to my temple clung, and stung
Again and again, digging in his hot lance.
I took him gently between my finger and thumb
And cast him against the air. He circled once
Glancing into the sun, then zoomed away.
There may be a moral here, though not for me;
But that is why, I think, I dream in this way,
Recalling things that nobody else would see.

Philip Hobsbaum

Traditional

toad

The 'ornet lived in an 'ollow tree.
A narsty spiteful twud were 'e.

Buzzing Death Of the many vicious pests of Northeastern India, the tree bee, half cousin of the Indian hornet, tops the list. These bees go about in immense swarms, making their hives in the highest trees. Unlike the hornet, which will sting only when thoroughly annoyed, the tree bee has the habit of swooping down in attacking thousands, for no apparent reason, and chasing one for his life.

One sunny morning, riding along a dusty cart track, I found myself, without the least warning, the centre of such an assault. The sky above me suddenly became thick with bees. With an icy shiver down my spine, I put my pony, Souvenir, to a gallop. Flight seemed the only hope of safety, but Souvenir's speed availed us nothing; the bees were after us in earnest. Souvenir jumped, bucked, reared and lashed out in all directions to rid himself of the bees, while I, attempting to protect my face and limbs, had the greatest difficulty in retaining my saddle. In a few moments, an angry buck while turning a corner at full gallop threw me into the dust.

With less than a mile to safety, I began to leg it with far greater determination than I had ever done in my life. But I was covered from head to foot with bees; they crawled in thousands all over me, stinging with excruciating pain. The under-rim of my topee became an angry hive, bees clustered inches deep. My forehead, ears and neck were blanketed in a buzzing, stinging swab of agony. Bees crawled inside my open-necked shirt and up my unprotecting shorts; they were everywhere. I tore them away in handfuls, but only to make room for others about me in clouds.

As I staggered on I yelled frantically to distant workers; but seeing the swarms about me, they bolted in every direction but mine. Gasping for breath, each time I opened my swollen mouth, more bees entered, until my tongue was stung to twice its normal size, and I was crunching them with my teeth. My nostrils had swollen into uselessness; my eyes, stung and running with water, were rapidly closing.

Stumbling weakly into the factory compound, I groped my way toward a building that was being erected. As soon as the men working there saw the droning battle array accompanying me, they made for cover at top speed. With the certainty of being half killed themselves, there was no alternative for them.

I was now a pitiful specimen, blind and deaf, and only able to breathe with extreme difficulty. Scrambling about with unseeing eyes ended by my falling unexpectedly into a huge heap of something soft and powdery, which I sensed must be a mound of red brick dust, used for building purposes. I quickly found myself in a worse quandary, brick dust choking out what little life I had remaining, and the angry swarm concentrating a renewed attack on my lower regions. Withdrawing from the brick dust, I used my remaining strength in a search for the water tank I knew was near. Staggering about in circles, I tore bees from my face and crushed them in handfuls, until I went down in a state of coma, powerless to defend myself. The bees had won.

After what seemed a lifetime, an unpleasant sensation of great heat swept over me. Presently I faintly felt the touch of human hands as rescuers hurried me away to safety. The reaction proved too strong, and I passed out.

My timely rescue was effected by two quick-witted Ghurkas, who had raced to a thatch stack and, bringing bundles of dry grass, had quickly surrounded me with a dense wall of fire and smoke, until the bees were beaten off. Later, as I lay unconscious, while the district was being scoured for a doctor, these same two staunch men insisted upon remaining and extracting stings from my inflamed carcass. It took two days to free my body of the discarded stings. When, eventually, I recovered consciousness I was beamingly informed that I had had at least two thousand punctures, probably a record.

I lay in torment for several days, unable to move. My body, blown up like an oversized sausage, was black, blue and purple, and as hard as frozen meat. For several days I could see and speak only with the greatest difficulty, and it took many applications of anti-swelling lotions before what had once been my nose and ears again emerged from the general mess.

My convalescence was a lengthy business of some six months in the hospital and several weeks in the cool hills of Darjeeling. When I returned to my old haunts I could never refrain from ducking and looking for the nearest cover whenever a droning swarm passed overhead.

J. W. Beagle-Atkins

Haiku
Translated from the
Japanese by R. H. Blyth
Issa

The aged dog
Seems impressed with the song
    Of the earthworms.

Esther's Tomcat

Daylong this tomcat lies stretched flat
As an old rough mat, no mouth and no eyes.
Continual wars and wives are what
Have tattered his ears and battered his head.

Like a bundle of old rope and iron
Sleeps till blue dusk. Then reappear
His eyes, green as ringstones: he yawns wide red,
Fangs fine as a lady's needle and bright.

A tomcat sprang at a mounted knight,
Locked round his neck like a trap of hooks
While the knight rode fighting its clawing and bite.
After hundreds of years the stain's there

On the stone where he fell, dead of the tom:
That was at Barnborough. The tomcat still
Grallochs odd dogs on the quiet,
Will take the head clean off your simple pullet,

disembowels

Is unkillable. From the dog's fury,
From gunshot fired point-blank, he brings
His skin whole, and whole
From owlish moons of bekittenings

Among ashcans. He leaps and lightly
Walks upon sleep, his mind on the moon.
Nightly over the round world of men,

Ted Hughes

Over the roofs go his eyes and outcry.

The Pet Shop

I never had the luck to keep a pet:
canary, rabbit, kitten, all were tried.
When she went mad, my father drowned the cat;
the rabbit fretted, the canaries died.

So, though my legs grew longer than my years,
I had no pup to race me round the hills.
The very sticklebacks brought home in jars,
within the week, were furred with fishy ills.

But when, on Saturdays, we went to town,
my chums and I, one window drew our gaze:
glass-tanks of snakes and lizards green and brown;
white mice and piebald mice on sawdust trays;
dumb tortoises; a haughty cockatoo;
bright-feathered bantams picking in the grit;
quick ferrets sniffing straw for something new,
and pigeons jerking on pink, clockwork feet.

Among the crowd that idled round the door,
you'd sometimes see a fellow slip his hand
into a hidden pocket to withdraw
a cowering lark or linnet contraband.

John Hewitt

```
chat
shah   shah
       chat
           chat   shah   cha   ha
           shah   chat   cha   ha
       shah
       chat
cha
cha

                              ha
                              chat
                              chat
                              chatshahchat
                     chachacha        chachacha
                        shahchatshah
                              shah
                              shah
                               ha
cha
cha
chatcha
     cha
     shahcha
         cha
         chatcha
             cha
             shahcha
                 cha
                 cha
                                              sh    ch
                                                aha
                                              ch    sh
```

French Persian Cats
Having a Ball
Edwin Morgan

66

The Parson's Eye-Lid and the Black Cat's Tail

11 March, Friday . . . The Stiony on my right Eye-lid still swelled and inflamed very much. As it is commonly said that the Eye-lid being rubbed by the tail of a black Cat would do it much good if not entirely cure it, and having a black Cat, a little before dinner I made a trial of it, and very soon after dinner I found my Eye-lid much abated of the swelling and almost free from Pain. I cannot therefore but conclude it to be of the greatest service to a Stiony on the Eye-lid. Any other Cat's Tail may have the above effect in all probability – but I did my Eye-lid with my own black Tom Cat's Tail . . . .

15 March, Tuesday . . . My right Eye again, that is, its Eye-lid much inflamed again and rather painful.

James Woodforde

Mending the Cat

26 October. I had a poor little cat, that had one of her ribs broke and that laid across her belly, and we could not tell what it was, and she was in great pain. I therefore with a small pen knife this morning, opened one side of her and took it out, and performed the operation very well, and afterwards sewed it up and put Friars Balsam to it, and she was much better after, the incision was half an inch. It grieved me much to see the poor creature in such pain before, and therefore made me undertake the above, which I hope will preserve the life of the poor creature.

James Woodforde

Horse   The horse at the shore
Casks of red apples, skull, a barrel of rum

The horse in the field
Plough, ploughman, gulls, a furrow, a cornstalk

The horse in the peat-bog
Twelve baskets of dark fire

The horse at the pier
Letters, bread, paraffin, one passenger, papers

The horse at the show
Ribbons, raffia, high bright hooves

The horse in the meadow
A stallion, a red wind, between the hills

George   The horse at the burn
Mackay Brown   Quenching a long flame in the throat

The Horse   Hast thou given the horse his might?
Hast thou clothed his neck with the quivering mane?
Hast thou made him to leap as a locust?
The glory of his snorting is terrible.
He paweth in the valley, and rejoiceth in his strength:
He goeth out to meet the armed men.
He mocketh at fear, and is not dismayed;
Neither turneth he back from the sword.
The quiver rattleth against him,
The flashing spear and the javelin.
He swalloweth the ground with fierceness and rage;
Neither believeth he that it is the voice of the trumpet.
As oft as the trumpet soundeth he saith, 'Aha!'
And he smelleth the battle afar off,
The Bible   The thunder of the captains, and the shouting.

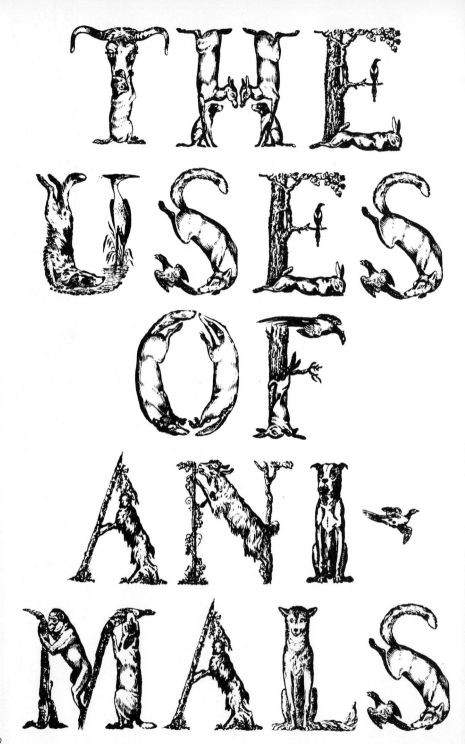

THE USES OF ANIMALS

Weather Rhymes

If clouds look as if scratched by a hen
Get ready to reef your topsails then.

If the cock goes crowing to bed,
He'll certainly rise with a watery head.

Woody Guthrie Talking

He was fightin' like a bee in under a horse's tail.

The Teacher asked me, 'If I lay one egg here on this desk,
and two over here on that table, how many eggs would that
be?' I told her, 'Just don't go countin' them eggs till you
lay 'em.'

Proverbs

A pig in armour is still a pig.

Birds that live in water are never wet.

Great cry but little wool, as the devil said when he sheared
his hogs.

If you cut down the forest, you'll catch the wolf.

Laws catch flies, but let hornets go free.

The dust raised by the sheep does not choke the wolf.

The dog in his kennel barks at his fleas, but the dog that
hunts doesn't feel them.

The kick of a camel is soft but stunning.

African Proverb

Becoming a chief's favourite
Is not always easy;
It is like making friends
With a hippopotamus.

Indian 'Sad Song'

Perching on a branch the fish-eagle looks about and cries
wildly; my heart too becomes restless at some unaccountable
feeling.

Song of the Battery Hen

We can't grumble about accommodation:
we have a new concrete floor that's
always dry, four walls that are
painted white, and a sheet-iron roof
the rain drums on. A fan blows warm air
beneath our feet to disperse the smell
of chicken-shit and, on dull days,
fluorescent lighting sees us.

You can tell me: if you come by
the North door, I am in the twelfth pen
on the left-hand side of the third row
from the floor; and in that pen
I am usually the middle one of three.
But, even without directions, you'd
discover me. I have the same orange-
red comb, yellow beak and auburn
feathers, but as the door opens and you
hear above the electric fan a kind of
one-word wail, I am the one
who sounds loudest in my head.

Listen. Outside this house there's an
orchard with small moss-green apple
trees; beyond that, two fields of
cabbages; then, on the far side of
the road, a broiler house. Listen:
one cockerel grows out of there, as
tall and proud as the first hour of sun.
Sometimes I stop calling with the others
to listen, and wonder if he hears me.

The next time you come here, look for me.
Notice the way I sound inside my head.
God made us all quite differently,
and blessed us with this expensive home.

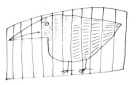

Edwin Brock

Is it cruel?

A Robin redbreast in a cage
Puts all heaven in a rage.
A dove-house filled with doves and pigeons
Shudders hell through all its regions.

William Blake

Or isn't it?
King Solomon's Ring
Konrad Lorenz

. . . it is no great act of cruelty to keep a nightingale or a
goldfinch alone in captivity for the purpose of its song and
Blake's adage need not be taken too seriously.

Hanno and Ping   It was morning in the Monkey House – one of those bitterly cold May days with driving snow that sometimes happen in an English summer. Through the grubby glass roof the colourless London light filtered down, helped by electricity to something approaching the gaiety of the inside of King's Cross station. The wide floor between the two rows of cages had been newly scrubbed and was as inviting as wet concrete ever is.

Through the door came an army of children enjoying a school treat. They fought to enter, were squeezed into eager immobility in the doorway, arms and legs locked, and burst yelling into the interior. Among them was a Chinese boy known to his friends as Ping, though that was not his real name. He was an orphan refugee living in a hostel. He was trim, self-possessed and gay, and he thought his own thoughts. Indeed he was so unlike his companions both in race and circumstance that his thoughts would scarcely have been understood or welcomed. His firm tight little mouth gave way to curled smiles which were all the more attractive because of the impression that only half the smile had been allowed out. He came through the door in a squeezing mass with the others, who ran shouting and pointing down the rows of cages, laughing and being peevishly answered back by the monkeys. Ping was no sooner inside than he was squirming with distaste. What had he in his innocence expected? A great pavilion full of palms, banana trees and giant ferns, streamers of orchids hanging down from the ceiling smelling of everything exotic, among which the monkeys peeped and sprang as gaily as at home? Before he had been displaced he had watched monkeys in his own forest as European children might watch squirrels in the New Forest, speckled with sun and shade, their bright eyes inquisitive and carefree. Certainly it had never occurred to him that an animal could be stripped of everything that went with it, of which its instincts were an inseparable part, and that you could have just its little body in a space of nothingness. As if looking at *that* told you anything but the nature of sorrow, which you knew anyway. Here in their ugly empty cages the monkeys were no more tropical than a collection of London rats or dirty park pigeons. They were degraded as in a slum. Some sat frowning with empty eyes, and those that wasted their unbelievable grace of movement in leaping from perch to chain, from chain to roof, from roof to perch to chain, repeating it for ever, had reduced to fidgety clockwork the limitless ballet of the trees which is vital joy.

Ping stood there saddened. He wanted to run out, but that was no good. What he really wanted was never to have come in. And then suddenly his attention was seized and he felt nothing but intense excitement. Ping had the kind of imagination that never dismisses anything as ordinary. Nothing was ordinary to him. What was always most surprising was just how extraordinary things are. It was hard to keep up with it. Now he saw in a special cage shut off from all the others, with a double row of bars between it and the public and plate glass round the outside as well, a stupendous black figure standing like a horse; like a horse that was also a man, for it had a man's brow and compelling and authoritative eyes, but its nostrils were large and soft like a horse's. Suddenly it sprang round facing him and stood upright. It *was* a man! It was a giant with a bare black chest ten times as wide as Ping's own. He could see the breaths it took.

This creature turned its back and walked to the rest of its cage where there was a step to a raised platform and a low door. Its legs were short in comparison with its size but very powerful, while the muscles of its back and shoulders were something Ping looked at and knew he failed to imagine properly. It was too much. It laid a hand on the platform and vaulted effortlessly up, turning round in the all-fours position to face Ping. Its attitude was that of whirlwind force held ready and very lightly triggered. It was listening intently and turned its magnificent crested head in quick jerks from side to side. Ping dropped his eyes for a second to read the label on the cage. He could not wait any longer to know.

HANNO
Gorilla Gorilla. Belgian Congo
Aged 13

Hanno took advantage of his raised position to hurl himself at the front of his cage. People scattered with cries of fright, but Ping gripped the rail, too rapt to move. Hanno's leaps were catapult-violent, but he landed in balance ready for another spring in any direction. After much leaping to and fro and up and down, and pressing his face to the bars in an effort to see further out sideways, while Ping stood just in front lost in admiration, Hanno walked across to a cast iron door leading to the Keeper's passage at one side of his cage. He tried it sharply to see if it was locked, as of course it was, and he knew that as well as anyone else. He then examined it all round the edge, prising and pushing with fingers as strong as tyre levers.

It would not budge. He flicked himself back against the opposite wall in a sidelong action of two legs and one arm, and turned to face the door. With a bound he was back upon it, standing erect to pound on the door with his fists. It was an expert smashing drum-roll, getting faster and faster, till he finished with both arms stylishly raised like a tympanist in a symphony who has just had his big moment, the final Boom! Boom! in this case CLANG CLANG. The Monkey House shook to the passionate gong. It was loud enough, one would have thought, to have halted the London traffic outside. Inside the chimpanzees began to imitate him, and to stamp and clap, and the other monkeys to scream.

The teacher was tugging at Ping's arm.

'We are going to the Lion House,' she yelled. 'Come along.'

A Stranger at
Green Knowe
L. M. Boston

Ping shook his head, then as the noise died down for a moment he said, still gazing at Hanno, 'I'm staying here.' Just in time he remembered his manners, turning with the little bow he still did unconsciously, 'Please.'

Finding the Gorilla Some two and a half hours after leaving the Rukumi meadow, I stood on the summit, marked by a shallow crater, a rain gauge, and an assortment of boards, cans, and other rubbish discarded by the many expeditions that had reached the top since the first climbers in 1903.

I waited twenty minutes for the clouds to disperse, but when it started to hail I hurried down the slope. I remembered the tragedy of the geologist Kirschstein who was surprised by a snow-storm while descending in February 1907. His porters, in snow and bitter cold for the first time in their lives, lay down and refused to get up again. They moaned, 'It is the decree of the gods – we must die.' Twenty porters died in that storm, and Kirschstein, in his effort to drag the half-frozen Africans to shelter, caught pneumonia and lay unconscious for two days.

Numerous deep ravines radiate from the summit like the spokes of a wheel. Unable to see more than fifty feet ahead, I did not follow the same path I used in climbing up. Far down the mountain I took a compass bearing and knew that I had strayed. I climbed in and out of ravines as I crossed the slope. clumps/shrubs The rock was wet and slippery, and the stands of senecios presented a chaotic mass of brittle stems that snapped underfoot, pitching me into the sodden moss that carpeted the ground. It was an eerie shadow-world, full of grotesque shapes, monsters that appeared for a moment only to vanish again. Suddenly a buffalo rose out of the swirling fog, standing there black and ominous, head slightly lowered to reveal the sweeping curve of its horns. I stopped until it disappeared soundlessly like a phantom. Only later, far away, I heard the breaking of branches.

When I reached the rest-house only a guard was waiting for me; the others had returned to Kabara. I stripped off my wet clothes and, wrapped in a blanket, squatted by the fire until darkness fell.

For the next two days we continued our search for gorillas. We found some fresh feeding sites, and Doc once thought he heard a gorilla in the distance. On the third day, far down along the Kanyamagufa Canyon, I heard a sound that electrified me – a rapid *pok-pok-pok*, the sound of a gorilla pounding its chest. I followed the edge of the canyon until I found a game trail that crossed it. Carefully I scouted along the slope where I expected the animal to be. But I had no luck. Only later did I learn that there is an almost ventriloquial quality in the sound of chest-beating that makes distance very difficult to judge.

When Doc and I returned to the canyon in the morning we were greeted by the same noise. Evidently a gorilla had spotted us. I climbed into the crown of a tree to look over the shrubs that obscured our view, and Doc circled up the slope. Suddenly, as he told me later, the undergrowth swayed forty feet ahead, and Doc heard the soft grumbling sound of contented animals. Unaware of him, the gorillas approached to within thirty feet. Two black, shaggy heads peered for ten seconds from the vegetation. Uncertain of how to react, Doc raised his arms. The animals screamed and walked away. We both examined the swathe of freshly trampled vegetation and the torn remnants of wild celery and nettles on which the gorillas had been feeding. While Doc took notes on the spoor, I followed the trail. The musty, somewhat sweet odour of gorilla hung in the air. Somewhere ahead and out of sight, a gorilla roared and roared again, *uuua-uuua!* an explosive, half-screaming sound that shattered the stillness of the forest and made the hairs on my neck rise. I took a few steps and stopped, listened, and moved again. The only sound was the buzzing of insects. Far below me white clouds crept up the slopes and fingered into the canyons. Then another roar, but farther away. I continued over a ridge, down, and up again. Finally I saw them, on the opposite slope about two hundred feet away, some sitting on the ground, others in trees.

An adult male, easily recognizable by his huge size and grey back, sat among the herbs and vines. He watched me intently and then roared. Beside him sat a juvenile perhaps four years old. Three females, fat and placid, with sagging breasts and long nipples, squatted near the male, and up in the fork of a tree crouched a female with a small infant clinging to the hair on her shoulders. A few other animals moved around in the dense vegetation. Accustomed to the drab gorillas in zoos, with their pelage lustreless and scuffed by the cement floors of their cages, I was little prepared for the beauty of the beasts before me. Their hair was not merely black, but a shining blue-black, and their black faces shone as if polished.

We sat watching each other. The large male, more than the others, held my attention. He rose repeatedly on his short, bowed legs to his full height, about six feet, whipped his arms up to beat a rapid tattoo on his bare chest, and sat down again. He was the most magnificent animal I had ever seen. His brow ridges overhung his eyes, and the crest on his crown resembled a hairy mitre; his mouth when he roared was cavernous, and the large canine teeth were covered with black tartar. He lay on the slope, propped on his huge shaggy arms, and the muscles of his broad shoulders and silver back rippled. He gave the impression of dignity and restrained power, of absolute certainty in his majestic appearance. I felt a desire to communicate with him, to let him know by some small gesture that I intended no harm, that I wished only to be near him. Never before had I had this feeling on meeting an animal. As we watched each other across the valley, I wondered if he recognized the kinship that bound us.

After a while the roars of the male became less frequent, and the other members of the group scattered slowly. Some climbed ponderously into shrubby trees and fed on the vines that draped from the branches; others reclined on the ground, either on the back or on the side, lazily reaching out every so often to pluck a leaf. They still kept their eyes on me, but I was amazed at their lack of excitement.

The Year of the Gorilla
George B. Schaller

Wolves Fighting

An enormous old timber wolf and a rather weaker, obviously younger one are the opposing champions and they are moving in circles round each other, exhibiting admirable 'footwork'. At the same time, the bared fangs flash in such a rapid exchange of snaps that the eye can scarcely follow them. So far, nothing has really happened. The jaws of one wolf close on the gleaming white teeth of the other who is on the alert and wards off the attack. Only the lips have received one or two minor injuries. The younger wolf is gradually being forced backwards. It dawns upon us that the older one is purposely manoeuvring him towards the fence. We wait with breathless anticipation what will happen when he 'goes to the wall'. Now he strikes the wire netting, stumbles . . . and the old one is upon him. And now the incredible happens, just the opposite of what you would expect. The furious whirling of the grey bodies has come to a sudden standstill. Shoulder to shoulder they stand, pressed against each other in a stiff and strained attitude, both heads now facing in the same direction. Both wolves are growling angrily, the elder in a deep bass, the younger in higher tones, suggestive of the fear that underlies his threat. But notice carefully the position of the two opponents; the older wolf has his muzzle close, very close against the neck of the younger, and the latter holds away his head, offering unprotected to his enemy the bend of his neck, the most vulnerable part of his whole body! Less than an inch from the tensed neck-muscles, where the jugular vein lies

immediately beneath the skin, gleam the fangs of his antagonist from beneath the wickedly retracted lips. Whereas, during the thick of the fight, both wolves were intent on keeping only their teeth, the one invulnerable part of the body, in opposition to each other, it now appears that the discomfited fighter proffers intentionally that part of his anatomy to which a bite must assuredly prove fatal. Appearances are notoriously deceptive, but in his case, surprisingly, they are not! . . .

Every second you expect violence and await with bated breath the moment when the winner's teeth will rip the jugular vein of the loser. But your fears are groundless, for it will not happen. In this particular situation, the victor will definitely not close on his less fortunate rival. You can see that he would like to, but he just cannot! A dog or wolf that offers its neck to its adversary in this way will never be bitten seriously. The other growls and grumbles, snaps with his teeth in the empty air and even carries out, without delivering so much as a bite, the movement of shaking something to death in the empty air. However, this strange inhibition from biting persists only so long as the defeated dog or wolf maintains his attitude of humility. Since the fight is stopped so suddenly by this action, the victor frequently finds himself straddling his vanquished foe in anything but a comfortable position. So to remain, with his muzzle applied to the neck of the 'under-dog', soon becomes tedious for the champion, and, seeing that he cannot bite anyway, he soon withdraws. Upon this, the under-dog may hastily attempt to put distance between himself and his superior. But he is not usually successful in this, for, as soon as he abandons his rigid attitude of submission, the other again falls upon him like a thunderbolt and the victim must again freeze into his former posture. It seems as if the victor is only waiting for the moment when the other will relinquish his submissive attitude, thereby enabling him to give vent to his urgent desire to bite. But, luckily for the 'under-dog', the top-dog at the close of the fight is overcome by the pressing need to leave his trade-mark on the battlefield, to designate it as his personal property – in other words, he must lift his leg against the nearest upright object. This right-of-possession ceremony is usually taken advantage of by the under-dog to make himself scarce.

King Solomon's Ring
Konrad Lorenz

How to Talk to Elephants

I was following the crest of a ridge along one of the many old elephant trails that criss-crossed the bamboo. Soon the tracks became fresh. The toe-nails were still clearly defined, and swarms of tiny black flies hovered about the heaps of dung. I pushed my fingers into some dung. It was still warm. Clouds drifted in, and grey fog crept from stem to stem, reducing my visibility to about fifty feet. I continued silently and carefully, straining my senses, trying to hear the swish of a branch, the rumble of a stomach, trying to see the bulky grey forms of the elephants in this shadowless, dusky world, trying to smell their musky odour. But the only sound was the pounding of my heart. I was afraid of stumbling upon the herd, for it would be dangerous to have to elude them in this fog. Finally I talked to them in a normal voice: 'Elephants, hallo. Please get off the trail. This ridge leads to my camp, and I don't want to leave it. I am only a human being, a weakling without weapons. I can do you no harm. Please leave the trail and let me pass.' And just ahead, without a sound, the elephants left the trail and angled into the valley.

The Year of the Gorilla
George B. Schaller

Elephants are Different to Different People

Wilson and Pilcer and Snack stood before the zoo elephant.

Wilson said, 'What is its name? Is it from Asia or Africa? Who feeds it? Is it a he or a she? How old is it? Do they have twins? How much does it cost to feed? How much does it weigh? If it dies, how much will another one cost? If it dies, what will they use the bones, the fat, and the hide for? What use is it besides to look at?'

Pilcer didn't have any questions; he was murmuring to himself, 'It's a house by itself, walls and windows, the ears come from tall cornfields, by God; the architect of those legs was a workman, by God; he stands like a bridge out across deep water; the face is sad and the eyes are kind; I know elephants are good to babies.'

Snack looked up and down and at last said to himself, 'He's a tough son-of-a-gun outside and I'll bet he's got a strong heart, I'll bet he's strong as a copper-riveted boiler inside.'

They didn't put up any arguments.

They didn't throw anything in each other's faces.

Three men saw the elephant three ways

And let it go at that.

They didn't spoil a sunny Sunday afternoon;

'Sunday comes only once a week,' they told each other.

Carl Sandburg

Pygmies' Elephant Song

On the weeping forest, under the evening wind,
Black night has lain down joyfully,
In the sky the stars have fled, trembling,
Fireflies that shine vaguely and go out.
Up there, the moon is dark, its white light has gone out.
The spirits are wandering.
Elephant hunter, take your bow!
Elephant hunter, take your bow!

In the frightened forest the tree sleeps, leaves are dead,
Monkeys have shut their eyes, hanging high in the branches,
Antelopes slip along with silent steps,
Crop the fresh grass, prick up their ears, intent,
Raise their head and listen, startled.
The cicada falls silent, shutting in its rasping song.
Elephant hunter, take your bow!
Elephant hunter, take your bow!

insect like a grasshopper

In the forest lashed by a great rain,
Father elephant walks, heavily, *bau, bau,*
At ease and fearless, sure of his strength,
Breaking through the forest, he stops, starts off again.
He eats, trumpets, knocks down tree, and seeks his mate.
Father elephant, you are heard from far away.
Elephant hunter, take your bow!
Elephant hunter, take your bow!

In the forest through which no man except you goes,
Hunter, lift up your heart, slip, run, jump, walk!
Meat is before you, the huge mass of meat,
The meat that walks like a hill,
The meat that makes the heart glad,
The meat that will roast at your fire,
The meat into which your teeth sink,
The fine red meat and the blood that is drunk smoking.
Elephant hunter, take your bow!
Elephant hunter, take your bow!

Translated from an African language by H. Trilles and Willard R. Trask
Traditional

Orpingalik's Song:
My Breath

(This is what I call this song, for it is just as necessary to me
to sing it as it is to breathe.)

I will sing a song,
A song that is strong.
    Unaya-unaya.

Sick I have lain since autumn,
Helpless I lay, as were I
My own child.

Sad, I would that my woman
Were away to another house
To a husband
Who can be her refuge,
Safe and secure as winter ice.
    Unaya-unaya.

Dost thou know thyself?
So little thou knowest of thyself.
Feeble I lie here on my bench
And only my memories are strong!
    Unaya-unaya.

Beasts of the hunt! Big game!
Often the fleeting quarry I chased!
Let me live it again and remember,
Forgetting my weakness.
    Unaya-unaya.

Let me recall the great white
Polar bear,
High up its back body,
Snout in the snow, it came!
He really believed
He alone was a male
And ran towards me.
    Unaya-unaya.

It threw me down
Again and again,
Then breathless departed
And lay down to rest,
Hid by a mound on a floe.
Heedless it was, and unknowing
That I was to be its fate.
Deluding itself
That he alone was a male,

And unthinking
That I too was a man!
    Unaya-unaya.

I shall ne'er forget that great blubber-beast,
A fjord seal,
I killed from the sea ice
Early, long before dawn,
While my companions at home
Still lay like the dead,
Faint from failure and hunger,
Sleeping.
With meat and with swelling blubber
I returned so quickly
As if merely running over ice
To view a breathing hole there.

And yet it was
An old and cunning male seal.
But before he had even breathed
My harpoon head was fast
Mortally deep in his neck.

That was the manner of me then.
Now I lie feeble on my bench
Unable even a little blubber to get
For my wife's stone lamp.
The time, the time will not pass,
While dawn gives place to dawn
And spring is upon the village.
    Unaya-unaya.

But how long shall I lie here?
How long?
And how long must she go a-begging
For fat for her lamp,
For skins for clothing
And meat for a meal?
A helpless thing – a defenceless woman.
    Unaya-unaya.

Knowest thou thyself?
So little thou knowest of thyself!
While dawn gives place to dawn,
And spring is upon the village.
    Unaya-unaya.

Translated from an
Eskimo dialect
by W. E. Calvert
Orpingalik

Device for a Hunter
Translated from a
Nigerian language by
Roger Rosfelder and
Willard R. Trask
Anonymous

It is not for the meat
But for the sport of it that we hunt.
If you think we are out for the meat,
We will go back!
Meat is something you find at home or at the butcher's.

How the Captain Got a Stiff Neck

Francis Kilvert

The Jacksons were there, Georgie and George Awdry with Miss Lucy Peck and the Frederick Awdrys with Capt. Hill, their cousin, a tall handsome powerful man who when tiger hunting once in India was seized by a tiger by the back of his neck. But he so pommelled the tiger's face over his shoulder that the beast let go, leaving Capt. Hill however with a stiff neck for life.

Hyena   I am waiting for you.
I have been travelling all morning through the bush

I am lying at the edge of the bush
stockade   on a dusty path that leads from the burnt-out kraal.
I am panting, it is midday, I found no water-hole.
I am very fierce without food and although my eyes
are screwed to slits against the sun
you must believe that I am ready to spring.

What do you think of me?
I have a rough coat like Africa.
I am crafty with dark spots
like the bush-tufted plains of Africa.
I sprawl as a shaggy bundle of gathered energy
like Africa sprawling in its waters.
I trot, I lope, I slaver, I am a ranger.
I hunch my shoulders. I eat the dead.

Do you like my song?
When the moon pours hard and cold on the veldt
I sing, and I am the slave of darkness.
Over the stone walls and the mud walls and the ruined places
and the owls, the moonlight falls.
I sniff a broken drum. I bristle. My pelt is silver.
I howl my song to the moon – up it goes.
Would you meet me there in the waste places?

It is said I am a good match
for a dead lion. I put my muzzle
at his golden flanks, and tear. He
is my golden supper, but my tastes are easy.
I have a crowd of fangs, and I use them.
Oh and my tongue – do you like me
when it comes lolling out over my jaw
very long, and I am laughing?
I am not laughing.
But I am not snarling either, only
panting in the sun, showing you
what I grip
carrion with.

I am waiting
for the foot to slide,
for the heart to seize,
for the leaping sinews to go slack,
for the fight to the death to be fought to the death,
for a glazing eye and the rumour of blood.
I am crouching in my dry shadows
till you are ready for me.
My place is to pick you clean

Edwin Morgan   and leave your bones to the wind.

The Third Day of the Wolf

Lock the gates and man the fences!
The lone Canadian timber-wolf
has escaped into the thickets, the ditches, the distances!
Blow the silver whistles!
The zoo-born sniffs the field mist,
the hedgerow leaves, liberty wind
of a cold February Friday.

D

Saturday trudging, loping, hungry, free but hunted,
dogs tracking, baying, losing scent, shouts dying,
fields dangerous, hills worse, night welcome, but the hunger
now! And Sunday many miles, risking farms, seen panting,
dodging the droning helicopter shadows,
flashing past gardens, wilder, padding along a highway,
twilight, sleepy birdsong, dark safety – till a car
catches the grey thing in its rushing headlights,
throws it to the verge, stunned, ruptured, living, lying,
fangs dimly scrabbling the roots of Hertfordshire.
The haze lifting, the head rising, the legs limping, the run
beginning again, with torches, whispers, smell of men and guns,
far off warning, nearer receding, wavering, waiting
for a whimper, a twig crack, a blood spot, finding them
and coming on, coming nearer to the starving meeting-place.
Breaking cover as had to be, on the icy morning of Monday,
Monday suddenly opening all its mouths, gulping
with fury at the weary fragment, farmers, keepers, police,
two planes diving again and again to drive it
in terror towards the guns, and the farm's pet collie
underling's   cornering it at last with the understrapper's yap.
The empty belly and mad yellow eyes
waiting for man were then shot,
not killed, then bludgeoned,
not killed, then shot,
and killed.

How strong man is
with his helicopters and his planes,
his radios and rifles!
What a god for a collie!
O wild things, wild things
take care, beware of him.
Man mends his fences.
Take care, take strength.
Take care of the warrant
for death. How good
he is at that,
with his dirty sack
ready to lay on you:
it is necessary.
But I have a warrant
to lay this too,
a wreath for wildness,
Edwin Morgan   timber-wolf, timber-wolf.

The Ghost of the Buffaloes

Last night at black midnight I woke with a cry,
The windows were shaking, there was thunder on high,
The floor was atremble, the door was ajar,
White fires, crimson fires, shone from afar.
I rushed to the dooryard. The city was gone.
My home was a hut without orchard or lawn.
It was mud-smear and logs near a whispering stream,
Nothing else built by man could I see in my dream . . .
Then . . .

Ghost-kings came headlong, row upon row,
Gods of the Indians, torches aglow.

They mounted the bear and the elk and the deer,
withered And eagles gigantic, aged and sere,
They rode long-horn cattle, they cried 'A-la-la.'
They lifted the knife, the bow, and the spear,
They lifted ghost-torches from dead fires below,
The midnight made grand with the cry 'A-la-la.'
The midnight made grand with a red-god charge,

A red-god show,
A red-god show,
'A-la-la, a-la-la, a-la-la, a-la-la.'

With bodies like bronze, and terrible eyes
mountain cat Came the rank and the file, with catamount cries,
Gibbering, yipping, with hollow-skull clacks,
Riding white broncos with skeleton backs,
Scalp-hunters, beaded and spangled and bad,
Naked and lustful and foaming and mad,
Flashing primeval demoniac scorn,
Blood-thirst and pomp amid darkness reborn,
Power and glory that sleep in the grass
While the winds and the shows and the great rains pass.

They crossed the gray river, thousands abreast,
They rode in infinite lines to the west,
Tide upon tide of strange fury and foam,
Spirits and wraiths, the blue was their home,
The sky was their goal where the star-flags were furled,
And on past those far golden splendors they whirled.
They burned to dim meteors, lost in the deep.
And I turned in dazed wonder, thinking of sleep.

And the wind crept by
Alone, unkempt, unsatisfied,
The wind cried and cried –
Muttered the massacres long past,
Buffaloes in shambles vast . . .
An owl said: 'Hark, what is a-wing?'
I heard a cricket carolling,
I heard a cricket carolling,
I heard a cricket carolling.

Then . . .
Snuffing the lightning that crashed from on high
Rose royal old buffaloes, row upon row.
The lords of the prairie came galloping by.
And I cried in my heart 'A-la-la, a-la-la,
A red-god show,
A red-god show,
A-la-la, a-la-la, a-la-la, a-la-la.'

Buffaloes, buffaloes, thousands abreast,
A scourge and amazement, they swept to the west.
With black bobbing noses, with red rolling tongues,
Coughing forth steam from their leather-wrapped lungs,

Cows with their calves, bulls big and vain,
Goring the laggards, shaking the mane,
Stamping flint feet, flashing moon eyes,
Pompous and owlish, shaggy and wise.
Like sea-cliffs and caves resounded their ranks
With shoulders like waves, and undulant flanks.

Tide upon tide of strange fury and foam,
Spirits and wraiths, the blue was their home,
The sky was their goal where the star-flags were furled,
And on past those far golden splendors they whirled.
They burned to dim meteors, lost in the deep,
And I turned in dazed wonder, thinking of sleep.

I heard a cricket's cymbals play,
A scarecrow lightly flapped his rags,
And a pan that hung by his shoulder rang,
Rattled and thumped in a listless way,
And now the wind in the chimney sang,
The wind in the chimney,
The wind in the chimney,
The wind in the chimney,
        Seemed to say:-
'Dream, boy, dream,
If you anywise can.
To dream is the work
Of beast or man.
Life is the west-going dream-storms' breath,
Life is a dream, the sigh of the skies,
The breath of the stars, that nod on their pillows
With their golden hair mussed over their eyes.'
The locust played on his musical wing,
Sang to his mate of love's delight.
nocturnal bird   I heard the whippoorwill's soft fret.
I heard a cricket carolling,
I heard a cricket carolling,
I heard a cricket say: 'Good night, good night,
Vachel Lindsay   Good night, good night . . . good night.'

Men have been in our woods

Men have been in our woods and killed our badgers. We have found the mother and babies ripped to pieces by dogs. We have found the sett dug out as well.

The children have known the badgers for three years and were very proud and happy when we saw they had four or five cubs this year. We children are shocked, disgusted, and horrified that grown-up people, who should set us an example, should kill and destroy these beautiful and harmless animals. These men are not primitive people who have to hunt for food. They call this destroying of life a sport. We think they are people who have not got enough good things to occupy themselves. We would want you to put this in your paper so that the men who did it may see how we feel about it, and this may save someone else's badgers from the dreadful fright and pain ours had.

Anthony Phillips (age 10), **Michael Hewitt** (10), **Nicholas Wilsdon** (11), **John Plested** (9), **Geoffrey Seligman** (11), **Iain Bratchie** (9), **Lise Svendsen** (11). (We wrote this ourselves and it is what we feel.) – From St Gorran School, Manaccan, Cornwall.

This letter appeared recently in our local paper. The children whose badgers were killed go to a rather special school. St Gorran lies at the head of a creek on the Helford River – one of the loveliest parts of Cornwall. You go down to it through winding lanes, where trees and may blossom meet overhead to make a green tunnel and where dark green water lies in pools, dreams, round with bluebells, at the heads of the creeks. We've never had such a year for blossom...

Badger-baiting still goes on in Cornwall, and you can find advertisements offering for sale 'terriers, proved badger-baiters'. It is a peculiar sport. The huntsmen dig the badger from the sett and then pull him out with a special pair of tongs. And then the animal, held by men, is ripped to pieces by the terriers. The St Gorran children found their badger, a repulsive mess of blood and fur, by its sett along with some of its cubs; but the others had vanished, possibly for training terriers. After the letter appeared, the corpse of the badger also disappeared.

Strange pagan tales persist about badgers here – of badgers killed on Easter Sunday, on the incoming tide, thrown on to midsummer bonfires. At one time I dismissed it all as fantasy in this day and age. But I have met people who swear this still goes on and who specify two particular villages. It is unlikely, though, that one would ever discover the truth.

However, the result of that particular night's work is liable to have repercussions. A Devon woman, Mrs Ruth Murray, who is writing a book on badgers, wants to use this incident as a test case to persuade the Government to make the badger a protected species. Some farmers say the badger is a pest, but its supporters swear it is harmless and both the Ministry of Agriculture and the Forestry Commission agree. The St Gorran children want to raise the money to offer a reward of £25 for information leading to the prosecution of the sportsmen involved. The League against Cruel Sports has actually offered £100 for such information.

Judith Cook

'It's a marvellous sport and not at all cruel'

But not all hares are good losers. Some go on squealing in the greyhound's jaws for fifteen seconds or more. Or they die, stretched and mangled – like this one last week – in a terrible tug-of-war. If the dogs are efficient and destruction means only a snarl and a snap, the watchers applaud with shrill cries of 'Oh, magnificent kill!' – marvelling perhaps at the dog's ability to avoid prolonging the death.

In the fields around Weston, near Letchworth, where North Herts Coursing Club held its monthly meeting on Wednesday, some hares escaped. When this happens, the coursing fraternity is not mean with its praise. 'We all like to see the hare escaping', declared a dog-owner at Weston. 'Some of those little fellows are jolly clever and the greyhounds very stupid.' Beaters drove a hare towards a spot where two greyhounds were concealed. When the hare was forty yards beyond this spot, the dogs were "slipped" by Mr David Green, a Stevenage publican. As they closed in at frantic speed, the hare twisted and turned in panic, finally plunging into a hedgerow and freedom.

Another hare – and two more dogs were 'slipped'. The pursuit was brief and the finish bloody. One set of jaws snapped a leg; another crushed the hare's back. The hare stopped squealing.

If agony is measured in time alone, then it did not last very long. And if cruelty is measured in the same way, then the savagery was quite ordinary. 'I've travelled all over the country "slipping" at meetings from the Isle of Wight to Inverness', said Mr Green. 'It's a marvellous sport and not at all cruel.'

Coursing supporters show few signs of worry over abolition attempts. 'Our club retains the distinction of hunting hares over members' own land', said Mr Green.

Last May, a Live Hare Coursing (Abolition) Bill, brought in by eleven M.P.s, was talked out when the second reading was moved. Since then a *Sunday Times* investigation showed that about one in four hares died in coursing and not one in ten as suggested by the National Coursing Club.

The abolitionists have not finally decided when the Bill will be reintroduced.

Anonymous

Your brilliant photograph of a hare-coursing kill last week, high-lighted an all too frequent occurrence in this callous sport. Very often after a long course the hounds are too tired to deal the stricken hare a killing bite, and I have frequently witnessed two dogs grabbing a hare almost simultaneously after which follows a contest for possession of the still-very-much-alive creature.

On the second day of last year's Waterloo Cup at Lydiate (Lancs.), a very tired greyhound finally managed to pin down the hare after a gruelling course of about three minutes; after a further minute I was amazed to see the quarry struggle free and limp away (the dog, presumably suffering from cramp, was unable to give further chase). The mutilated hare stumbled on only yards from the crowd and not one person tried to put it out of its misery.

On the other hand there was great concern for the dog whose female handler was almost in tears. The woman wrapped a blanket round her charge and smiled bravely as she turned to the crowd.

Meanwhile the other participant in this macabre little scene was seen to topple into a ditch and left to drown. Compassion it seems varies in direct proportion to the value in cash the animal is worth. – **John C. Burns,** Formby, Lancs.

While it would be ludicrous to pretend that coursing is a benign pursuit, there are far worse cruelties and indignities perpetrated upon animals for our supposed good. Moreover, if three out of four hares escape this is by no means a bad percentage. No vivisected dogs escape. No battery hens escape. – **J. West,** London W13.

The two dogs in your picture, were, from their posture, *not* 'tugging' away from each other. Dogs pull with out-stretched head. The hare appears neither stretched nor injured. The black dog was biting strongly the neck or upper spine – the action that kills immediately. This hare was evidently either being swiftly killed, or had been so a moment before.

Squealing is no proof of pain – as hares and rabbits yell even if touched, and some dogs can hold a hare without injury – or even of consciousness. Coursed hares are sold for human consumption, and are not mangled and uneatable. Hares 'twist and turn' because that is their natural action; wild animals pursued by predators do not panic or they would never survive.

The National Coursing Club always said kills could average at least 25 per cent in certain conditions; but they can also average less than two in ten (e.g., Waterloo Cup first day) or even five in forty-eight at one meeting. – **(Mrs) G. Flynn,** London SW1.

Letters to the Editor

One reads such articles and is shocked. It's outrageous! It ought to be stopped! Familiar reactions, but how does one go about stopping this kind of cruelty? Write to the papers expressing disgust at the inhumanity of people who perpetrate these horrors in the name of 'sport'? The people who act in this manner probably do not bother to read the letters and, if they do, the reading of them is hardly likely to have any effect.

It is the ordinary decent reader who can help – those who read, shudder and stick the article away out of reach of the children. If each of them would write to his M.P. urging support for the Live Hare Coursing (Abolition) Bill when next the Bill is reintroduced, perhaps these articles would soon be no longer necessary. – **Irene Dawson,** Marazion, Cornwall.

Your picture made me cry, and the accompanying caption made me sick to my stomach with angry rage. Rage because I personally can do so little to stop the appalling cruelty that is enacted daily in our so-called animal-loving country.

Can't we have a really militant group for the abolition of senseless cruelty that masquerades under the name of sport? Can't the Bill to abolish hare coursing be reintroduced? Must the destruction and suffering to all our wildlife – otters, foxes and hares – be allowed to continue?

Nature and wildlife is so much more worthy of preservation especially in our steel and concrete society. – **Catherine Spencer,** London W2.

Hares cannot be allowed to breed without any control. As they are animals that live above ground and mainly in the open, they cannot be gassed like foxes, rabbits and badgers. Neither can they be poisoned nor trapped. The only alternative to coursing is shooting.

I wonder how many of your readers have ever attended a hare shoot? Whether they have seen the wholesale slaughter, seen the half-dead hares flung into a truck to lie struggling and kicking until they finally die? Or have witnessed hares that have been shot and maimed but still manage to keep running – only to die a slow and lingering death by gangrene or starvation or at the hand of some predator?

Perhaps you feel this is better than to die in the jaws of two greyhounds or whippets in, as you state, a maximum of fifteen seconds – that is if the hare is unlucky and the greyhounds not experts. – **Susan Baird,** Crowborough.

Would hare-coursing enthusiasts be interested in widening the appeal of their sport?

This is how I see the variation. We get a group of stout-limbed chaps (preferably dressed in black leather) carrying stout sticks and capable of making a lot of noise. They crash through the homes of members of the National Coursing Club and drive members of the family into a field – preferably bowl-shaped so that we could all get a good view.

Two sporting tigers are 'slipped' and we applaud the chase and time the kill – at the same time remembering that we would all like to see the N.C.C. members escape. After all, some of those little fellows are very clever and the tigers (although acting instinctively) very stupid.

I admit that this is based on an idea about 2,000 years old but it would be a marvellous sport and not at all cruel. – **Clive Willis,** Esher.

Scene: A sandy hillock – Various holes, etc.

Beetles are quarrelling over a *Chrysalis*, which is seized first
by one then the other.

CHRYSALIS The whole world is bursting into blossom. I am
being born.

TRAMP *[Raising his head – he is lying half asleep]* How much?

CHRYSALIS The Great Adventure begins.

TRAMP Right oh! *[Settles down again.]*

[Pause]

MR BEETLE *[Behind the scenes]* What yer getting at?

MRS BEETLE *[Behind the scenes]* Me?

MR BEETLE Yes, you – you lump of rubbish.

MRS BEETLE Silly swine.

MR BEETLE Fathead.

MRS BEETLE Fathead yourself – mind where you're going.

[They enter, rolling a huge ball of dirt]

MR BEETLE It's all right, isn't it?

MRS BEETLE I'm all of a tremble.

MR BEETLE Our capital – that's what it is – our lovely capital –
careful – careful.

MRS BEETLE Can't be too careful with our capital – our
little pile.

MR BEETLE How we've saved and scraped and toiled and
moiled to come by it.

MRS BEETLE Night and morning, toiled and moiled and saved
and scraped.

MR BEETLE And we've seen it grow and grow, haven't we, bit
by bit – our little ball of blessedness.

MRS BEETLE Our very own it is.

MR BEETLE Our very own.

MRS BEETLE Our life's work.

MR BEETLE Smell it, old woman – pinch it – feel the weight
of it. Ours – ours.

MRS BEETLE A godsend.

MR BEETLE A blessing – straight from Heaven – capital –
capital.

CHRYSALIS Eternal night is breaking:
    The universe is waking:
    One minute, just one minute
    And I – *I* – shall be in it.

MRS BEETLE Husband.

MR BEETLE What is it, old woman?

MRS BEETLE Ha, ha, ha!

MR BEETLE Ha, ha, ha! Wife!

MRS BEETLE What is it, old man?

MR BEETLE Ha, ha! It's fine to own something – property – the dream of your life, the fruit of your labours.

MRS BEETLE Ha, ha, ha!

MR BEETLE I'm off my head with joy – I'm going barmy.

MRS BEETLE Why?

MR BEETLE With worry. Now we've got our little pile that we've so looked forward to, we've got to work and work and work to make another one.

MRS BEETLE Why another one?

MR BEETLE Silly – so that we can have two, of course.

MRS BEETLE Two? Quite right – quite right – two.

MR BEETLE Just fancy – two – at least two, say three. Every one who's made his pile has to make another.

MRS BEETLE So that he can have two?

MR BEETLE Yes, or three.

MRS BEETLE Husband.

MR BEETLE Well, what is it?

MRS BEETLE I'm scared – S'posin' some one was to steal it from us.

MR BEETLE What?

MRS BEETLE Our capital – our little pile – our all in all.

MR BEETLE Our pi-ile – My gawd – don't frighten me.

MRS BEETLE We oughtn't to roll it about with us till we've made another one, dearie, did we?

MR BEETLE I'll tell you what – we'll invest it – In – vest it – store it up – bury it. That's what we'll do – nice and deep – nice and deep.

MRS BEETLE I hope nobody finds it.

MR BEETLE Eh, what's that? Finds it – No, of course they won't. Our little bit of capital.

MRS BEETLE Our nest-egg – Oh, bless me – I hope no one does – our little all.

MR BEETLE Wait – stay here and watch it – Watch it careful – don't let your eyes off it, not for a minute – Capital – Capital.

MRS BEETLE Where yer off to?

MR BEETLE To look for a hole – a little hole – a deep hole – deep and narrer to bury it in – out of harm's way – Careful – Careful. [Exit]

MRS BEETLE Husband – husband, come back – wait a bit – I've found one – such a nice hole – Husband! He's gone! If I could only look into it – No, I mustn't leave yer. But only a peep – Here, stay here good and quiet, darling.

Hubby'll be back soon – in half a jiff, half a jiff – So long, keep good – half a ji –

[Enters the lair of the Ichneumon Fly]

CHRYSALIS Oh, to be born – to be born – into the great new world.

[Enter a Strange Beetle]

STRANGE BEETLE They've gone – now's my chance.

[Rolls pile away].

TRAMP 'Ere, mind where yer going to.

STRANGE BEETLE Mind yer feet.

TRAMP What's that yer rolling?

STRANGE BEETLE Ha, ha! That's my capital – my little pile, my all.

TRAMP Bit niffy, ain't it?

STRANGE BEETLE Eh?

TRAMP It smells.

STRANGE BEETLE Capital don't smell – Off you go, my precious – This way, my little all, my nest-egg, my capital. *[Exit]*

MRS BEETLE Oh dear, oh dear. That's somebody's house, that is – We can't put you there, my jewel. Oh, where's it gone to? Where's it gone to? My little pile – where's it gone to?

TRAMP Why, not 'arf a minute –

MRS BEETLE *[Rushing at him]* Thief – thief – What 'ave you done with my pile?

TRAMP I'm telling yer.

MRS BEETLE Here, give it back – yer wretch.

TRAMP Just this minute a gentleman rolled it away over there.

MRS BEETLE What gentleman? Who?

TRAMP A pot-bellied fellow, a fat, round chap.

MRS BEETLE My husband?

TRAMP A feller with an ugly mug and crooked feet.

MRS BEETLE That's my husband.

TRAMP His capital he said it was.

MRS BEETLE That's him – he must have found a hole – Husband – My precious – Darling! Where is the blasted fool?

TRAMP That's where he rolled it to.

MRS BEETLE Coo-eh! Couldn't he have called me? Husband, my precious! I'll learn yer – Our capital – our all – our little pile. *[Exit]*

TRAMP Them butterflies was gay
    And foolish, yer might say:

But these 'ere beetles – lumme,
They *do* work, anyway!
So, 'ere's to wish 'em luck –
Though gatherin' balls of muck
Is jest about as rummy
As anythink I've struck.

CHRYSALIS O universe, prepare! O space, expand! The
mightiest of all happenings is at hand.

TRAMP What's that?

CHRYSALIS I'm being born.

TRAMP That's good – and what are you going to be?

CHRYSALIS I don't know – I don't know – Something great.

TRAMP Ah, ha!

CHRYSALIS I'll do something extraordinary – I'm being born.

TRAMP What *you* want's life, my son.

CHRYSALIS When half a minute's gone,
                Something immense, unbounded,
        Will happen here.

TRAMP   Go on!

CHRYSALIS I shall do something great!

TRAMP What?

*Translated from
the Czech by P. Selver*
Karel Čapek

CHRYSALIS When I change my state,
        The world will be astounded!

TRAMP Well – 'urry up. I'll wait.

Boasting

'I'm shaggy as a bear, wolfish about the head, active as a cougar, and can grin like a hyena, until the bark will curl off a gum log. There's a sprinkling of all sorts in me, from the lion down to the skunk; and before the war is over, you will pronounce me an entire zoological institute, or I miss a figure

Davy Crockett in my calculation.'

Boasting

A: I am a man; I am a horse; I am a team. I can whip any man in all Kentucky, by God.

B: I am an alligator; half man, half horse; can whip any man on the Mississippi, by God.

A: I am a man; have the best horse, best dog, best gun, and handsomest wife in all Kentucky, by God.

B: I am a Mississippi snapping turtle; have bear's claws, alligator's teeth, and the devil's tail; can whip any man,

Traditional by God.

Wilderness

There is a wolf in me . . . fangs pointed for tearing gashes . . . a red tongue for raw meat . . . and the hot lapping of blood – I keep this wolf because the wilderness gave it to me and the wilderness will not let it go.

There is a fox in me . . . a silver-gray fox . . . I sniff and guess . . . I pick things out of the wind and air . . . I nose in the dark night and take sleepers and eat them and hide the feathers . . . I circle and loop and double-cross.

There is a hog in me . . . a snout and a belly . . . a machinery for eating and grunting . . . a machinery for sleeping satisfied in the sun – I got this too from the wilderness and the wilderness will not let it go.

There is a fish in me . . . I know I came from salt-blue water-gates . . . I scurried with shoals of herring . . . I blew waterspouts with porpoises . . . before land was . . . before the water went down . . . before Noah . . . before the first chapter of Genesis.

There is a baboon in me . . . clambering-clawed . . . dog-faced . . . yawping a galoot's hunger . . . hairy under the armpits . . . here are the hawk-eyed hankering men . . . here are the blonde and blue-eyed women . . . here they hide curled asleep waiting . . . ready to snarl and kill . . . ready to sing and give milk . . . waiting – I keep the baboon because the wilderness says so.

uncouth fellow

There is an eagle in me and a mockingbird . . . and the eagle flies among the Rocky Mountains of my dreams and fights among the Sierra crags of what I want . . . and the mockingbird warbles in the early forenoon before the dew is gone, warbles in the underbrush of my Chattanoogas of hope, gushes over the blue Ozark foothills of my wishes – And I got the eagle and the mockingbird from the wilderness.

O, I got a zoo, I got a menagerie, inside my ribs, under my bony head, under my red-valve heart – and I got something else: it is a man-child heart, a woman-child heart: it is a father and mother and lover: it came from God-Knows-Where: it is going to God-Knows-Where – For I am the keeper of the zoo: I say yes and no: I sing and kill and

Carl Sandburg work: I am a pal of the world: I came from the wilderness.

To a Fish You strange, astonished-looking, angle-faced,
    Dreary-mouthed, gaping wretches of the sea,
    Gulping salt-water everlastingly,
Cold-blooded, though with red your blood be graced,
And mute, though dwellers in the roaring waste;
    And you, all shapes besides, that fishy be, –
    Some round, some flat, some long, all devilry,
Legless, unloving, infamously chaste; –

creatures O scaly, slippery, wet, swift, staring wights,
    What is't ye do? What life lead? eh, dull goggles?
How do ye vary your vile days and nights?
    How pass your Sundays? Are ye still but joggles
In ceaseless wash? Still nought but gapes, and bites,
    And drinks, and stares, diversified with boggles?

A Fish Answers

Amazing monster! that, for aught I know,
    With the first sight of thee didst make our race
    For ever stare! O flat and shocking face,
Grimly divided from the breast below!
Thou that on dry land horribly dost go
    With a split body and most ridiculous pace,
    Prong after prong, disgracer of all grace,
Long-useless-finned, haired, upright, unwet, slow!
O breather of unbreathable, sword-sharp air,
    How canst exist? How bear thyself, thou dry
And dreary sloth? What particle canst share
    Of the only blessed life, the watery?
I sometimes see of ye an actual *pair*
    Go by! linked fin by fin! most odiously.

Leigh Hunt

Dunce Song

Then I'll be four-footed,
And modest with fur.
All over, all under,
Seemly and still.

Then I'll be patient:
A part of the ground.
I will go slowly,
And lowly - oh, sweet.

Then I'll be one of them
He that made all
Looks after the longest,
And tenderest loves.

Then I'll be quiet -
You can be quick -
And lie down all summer,
All winter, and sleep.

This dunce believes what no intelligent person can
believe, that he might become an animal. I'm sure it's
a very deep desire in every human being to be an animal.
We can't. We're not animals and never were, but many of
us long to be. The chief basis for our longing is the desire
to sleep as much as animals do. Every human being caught
taking a nap is ashamed. No animal is. That's just one
of the advantages of being an animal. Another advantage

Mark Van Doren   is that he has fur all over him.

Palmstroem in Animal Costume

Palmstroem loves to copy animal creatures,
and he trains two youthful tailors
specially to make him animal costumes.

Thus, e.g., he likes to perch as raven
in the upper branches of an oak tree
and to watch there the horizon.

Often, too, as St Bernard he
lays his shaggy head on valiant forepaws,
barks when sleeping, dreams of rescued travelers.

Or he spins a cobweb in his garden
using string, and sits there as a spider
many days within its center.

Or as carp with goggle eyes he splashes
in a circle round the fish pond's fountain
and permits the boys and girls to feed him.

Translated from the
German by Max Knight
Christian
Morgenstern

Or he hangs, dressed up in stork attire,
underneath the cabin of an airship
and thus travels forth to Egypt.

The End

Francis Kilvert

Old William also told the story of how old Squire Sadler Gale of Bulwich House at Allington made himself wings and flew off the garden wall. 'Watch I vlee!' he cried to the people. Then he dashed down into the horsepond.

Acknowledgements

For permission to use copyright material acknowledgement is made to the following:

Poems and Prose

For 'Buzzing Death' from *Tea Pests* by J. Beagle-Atkins to the author and William Blackwood & Sons Ltd; for the translations of 'We listen to insects', 'The Butterfly', 'An Exhausted Sparrow', 'The Swallow', 'Sneezing' and 'The Aged Dog' from *Haiku*, vols. 1–4, to R. H. Blyth and the Hokuseido Press; for 'Hanno and Ping' from *A Stranger at Green Knowe* by L. M. Boston to the author and Faber & Faber Ltd; for 'Song of the Battery Hen' by Edwin Brock to the author; for 'I am the Slowworm' from *Briggflatts* by Basil Bunting to the author and the Fulcrum Press; for 'Orpingalik's Song: My Breath' translated by W. E. Calvert from *Unwritten Song* edited by Willard R. Trask to the Macmillan Company of New York; for 'Creepers and Crawlers' from *The Insect Play* by Karel Čapek to the Estate of Karel Čapek and the Oxford University Press; for 'Boy and a Butterfly' by Phillip Chappell to the author; from 'Snakes from *John Clare: Selected Poems and Prose* edited by Eric Robinson and Geoffrey Summerfield to the Oxford University Press; for 'Men have been in our woods and have killed our badgers' by Judith Cook to the author; for 'The Soft Voice of the Serpent' by Nadine Gordimer from *The Soft Voice of the Serpent and Other Stories* to the author; for 'The Pet Shop' from *Collected Poems 1932–1967* by John Hewitt to the author and MacGibbon & Kee; for 'Tadpole Time' from *A Kestrel for a Knave* by Barry Hines to the author and Michael Joseph Ltd; for 'A Country Matter' by Philip Hobsbaum from *Winter's Tales for Children*, vol. 3, to the author and Macmillan & Co. Ltd; for 'I could have told you a lot of queer things' from *A Shepherd's Life* by W. H. Hudson to the author and Methuen & Co. Ltd; for 'Capturing a Fox' from *Poetry in the Making* by Ted Hughes to the author and Faber & Faber Ltd; for 'The Thought-Fox' from *The Hawk in the Rain* by Ted Hughes to the author, Faber & Faber Ltd and Harper & Row Inc.; for 'Esther's Tomcat' from *Lupercal* by Ted Hughes to the author and Faber & Faber Ltd; for 'Rook-Shooting', 'The Fire-Engine and the Jackdaws', 'How the Captain got a Stiff Neck' and 'The End' from *Kilvert's Diary* edited by William Plomer to the editor, Mrs G. J. K. Fletcher and Jonathan Cape Ltd; for 'Talking to a Butterfly' by Rudyard Kipling to Mrs George Bambridge and Macmillan & Co. Ltd; for 'At the Housefly Plant' and 'Palmstroem in Animal Costume' by Christian Morgenstern from *Gallows Songs* translated by Max Knight to the author and the University of California Press; for 'Hedgehogs in Heaven' by Richard Liebich to the author and Methuen & Co. Ltd; for 'The Ghost of the Buffaloes' by Vachel Lindsay from *Unwritten Song*, edited by Willard R. Trask, to the Macmillan Company of New York; for 'Or isn't it?' and 'Wolves fighting' from *King Solomon's Ring* by Konrad Lorenz to the author and Methuen & Co. Ltd; for 'Horse' from *Scottish Poetry 1* to George Mackay Brown and the Edinburgh University Press; for 'Snake-Phobia' by Alan

123

Moorehead to the author, Laurence Pollinger Ltd and the *Sunday Times;* for 'Orgy', 'The Chaffinch Map of Scotland', 'French Persian Cats having a Ball' and 'The Third Day of the Wolf' from *The Second Life* by Edwin Morgan to the author and the Edinburgh University Press; for 'Heron' and 'Hyena' by Edwin Morgan to the author; for 'The Fly' by T. Muffet from *The History of Four-footed Beasts* to the Da Capo Press; for 'The Naming of Insects' from *Ounce, Dice, Trice* by Alastair Reid to the author, Laurence Pollinger Ltd, J. M. Dent & Sons Ltd and Little, Brown & Co.; for 'A Goldwing Moth' and 'Wilderness' from *Cornhuskers* by Carl Sandburg to the author and Holt, Rinehart & Winston Inc.; for 'Elephants are Different to Different People' from *Home Front Memo* by Carl Sandburg to the author and Harcourt, Brace & World Inc.; for 'Finding the Gorilla' and 'How to Talk to Elephants' from *The Year of the Gorilla* by George B. Schaller to the author and William Collins & Sons Ltd; for 'The Cave' by Clive Spinage to the author; for 'The Horse' from *The Bible Designed to be read as Literature* by Ernest Sutherland Bates to the author, Laurence Pollinger Ltd, William Heinemann Ltd and Simon & Schuster Inc.; for 'Feel Like a Bird' from *To Mix with Time* by May Swenson to the author and Charles Scribner's Sons; for 'Hedgehog' from *The Owl in the Tree* by Anthony Thwaite to the author and the Oxford University Press; for 'Mass Killings' and 'The Raven' from *Tracks* by E. A. R. Ennion and N. Tinbergen to the authors and the Clarendon Press; for 'The Hedgehog' by E. Topsell from *The History of Four-Footed Beasts* to the Da Capo Press; for 'The Locust', 'Pygmies' Elephant Song' and 'Device for a Hunter' from *Unwritten Song,* edited by Willard R. Trask, to the Macmillan Company of New York; for 'The Menagerie at Versailles in *1775*' from *Telephone Poles* by John Updike to the author and André Deutsch Ltd; for 'Dunce Song' from *Collected and New Poems 1924-1963* by Mark Van Doren to the author and Hill & Wang Inc.; for 'Observing Flies' by Gilbert White to the Chiswick Press; for 'The Parson's Eye-Lid and the Black Cat's Tail' and 'Mending the Cat' from *Diary of a Country Parson 1785-1802* by James Woodforde to the Oxford University Press.

Pictures For the pictures on page 8 to André Kertesz from Magnum Photos; pages 10-11, 42-3, 63, 77 to Keystone Press Agency Ltd; pages 12-13, 84-5 to the Trustees of the British Museum; pages 20-1, 38-9, 100-101 to the Clarendon Press; page 23 to Kenneth Moreman and to the University of Utrecht Museum; page 26 to Little, Brown & Co.; pages 28-9 to André Deutsch Ltd; pages 34-5 to Radio Times Hulton Picture Library; pages 36-7, 94-5 to Ludi Blum; pages 44, 46, 57, 60 to Paul Popper Ltd; pages 53, 55, 73 to Camera Press; page 56 to Leonard G. Appleby; pages 58-9 to Clive Spinage; page 69 to the Royal Library, Windsor; page 65 to SPADEM; page 72 to Hamish Hamilton; page 81 to Methuen & Co. Ltd; pages 83, 91, 97 to the Victoria and Albert Museum; page 88 to the Holman Eskimo Cooperative; pages 90, 121 to the West Baffin Eskimo Cooperative Limited; pages 92-3 to the Kunsthistorisches Museum, Vienna; page 99 to Syndication International; page 105 to Tony Shipton; page 107 to Topix; page 116 to John Walmsley; pages 118-19 to Geoffrey Drury; page 122 to the Mansell Collection.

List of Illustrations

Index of Animals

Index of Authors, Translators and Collectors